BEN RATLIFF has been a jazz and pop critic for *The New York Times* since 1996. He has written three books: *The Jazz Ear: Conversations Over Music* (2008); *Coltrane: The Story of a Sound* (2007, finalist for the National Book Critics Circle Award); and *Jazz: A Critic's Guide to the 100 Most Important Recordings* (2002). He lives with his wife and two sons in the Bronx.

Additional Praise for *Every Song Ever*

"A remarkable new book . . . [Ratliff] goes leaping from Beethoven to Big Black, from Morton Feldman to Curtis Mayfield, identifying continuities while delighting in contrasts." —Alex Ross, *The New Yorker*

"What is remarkable about Ratliff . . . is his musical intelligence and his almost singular breadth of knowledge and sympathy for all kinds of music. He also writes very well, a quality not at all common among those who write about music in general, a famously tricky subject. . . . [Ratliff's] takes on various performances, recorded or live, are often unpredictable, never pedantic or exhibitionistic, and in every case informative." —August Kleinzahler, *The New York Times Book Review*

"Ratliff proposes new routes across the teeming landscape: modes of attentive listening based on concepts or musical properties. . . . Close listening is Mr. Ratliff's forte. . . . [He] leans toward nontechnical terms and unshowy language, which he then nudges toward the profound or revealing. . . . Readers will often find themselves propelled to YouTube or Spotify to hear what he's writing about." —Simon Reynolds, *The New York Times*

"The spectacle of an active mind processing a world in constant flux . . . Maybe, as Ratliff beautifully argues, the brooding aggression of metal obscures a deeper melancholy." —Hua Hsu, *The New Yorker*

"Ratliff continually brings things down to Earth, thanks in part to his inclusive spirit and his masterful way of translating music through words. . . . [His] exquisite language serves as a guide, revealing new ways to look at old favorites and spurring on explorations into songs unknown." —Ryan Dombal, *Pitchfork*

"The pleasure of reading great music criticism—which *Every Song Ever* is—lies in following a seasoned explorer who unearths the hidden passageways amid music's intricate systems of interlocking tunnels. Ratliff's musical mind is as sharp as his musical tastes are catholic, and he switches theoretical approaches as quickly as he shuffles through a century's worth of recorded music.... The connections that arise from Ratliff's exploratory methodology are at turns poetic and revelatory, and most certainly are not what ends up on the average playlist."   —Eric Harvey, *The New Republic*

"[Ratliff] reminds us, as he proceeds, of how urgently we need adventurous critics like him at a time when the notion of musical discovery has been appropriated by tech companies and sidelined in the chase for clicks.... He wants to offer all readers a way to appreciate, even love, songs that no right-functioning recommendation engine would ever put in their earbuds.... Ratliff celebrates the virtues of play and resistance, and knows that just as stabbing at a single note can fend off easy enchantment, so can seeking out lots of different sounds. It's a quest that just might expand your definitions of 'great music' in directions and at a rate you never thought possible."
                                  —Spencer Kornhaber, *The Atlantic*

"[An] illuminating and thought-provoking book ... In twenty beautifully rendered essays on subjects like repetition, slowness, speed, sadness, virtuosity, improvisation, loudness, and intimacy, Ratliff establishes provocative and thoroughly unexpected connections between genres.... Time and again, Ratliff, a master of enlightened juxtaposition, discovers connections that leave one mesmerized."
                                  —Jonathan Rosenberg,
                                  The Christian Science Monitor

"*Every Song Ever* jumps into the grand adventure of losing yourself in music, at a time when the technology boundaries have blown wide open. Ben Ratliff brilliantly makes connections between the arcane and the everyday, pointing to sounds you've never heard—as well as finding new pleasures in music you thought you'd already used up."

—Rob Sheffield, author of *Love Is a Mix Tape*
and *Turn Around Bright Eyes*

"Everyone knows we live in an age when most people can listen to anything, anytime, anywhere. Whether that's depressing or mind-expanding depends ultimately on what kind of attention we pay. Ben Ratliff has the gifts to help us surf this wave of sonic information, not stand there mumbling at it in a grumpy-grampy way. After all, it's presumably not going to end until the electrical grid does."

—John Jeremiah Sullivan, author of *Pulphead*

"This is a book about one exemplary listener's love for how many ways music can mean, set in sentences as forceful and subtle as Elvin Jones's drumming. Slayer and Shostakovich, Ali Akbar Khan and the Allman Brothers—none of them are the same once Ben Ratliff's ears get through with them. And your ears won't be the same once you get through *Every Song Ever*." —Michael Robbins, author of
Alien vs. Predator and *The Second Sex*

"[Ratliff] has a knack for articulating how a song works. . . . [He is] like a learned record-store sage, at once a ranter and a crowd-pleaser. . . . It's to his credit that he asks so many questions, offering a model of music appreciation that feels engaged and expansive. But perhaps the most galvanizing aspect of his project is that it leaves room for the DIY spirit to reemerge. . . . [*Every Song Ever*] reignites our sense of longing for connection, allowing us to roam more consciously through the infinite channels online." —David O'Neill, *Bookforum*

"Ratliff breaks down the act of listening to music into twenty distinct chapters, making perceptive connections between artists ranging from Shostakovich to Ali Akbar Khan to the Jackson 5. . . . [*Every Song Ever*] is filled with bold statements, close listenings, and playlists, and will be immensely rewarding for those who stick with it."

—Ben Segedin, *Booklist*

"Writing about music (not lyrics) isn't easy, and few do it as well as Ratliff. . . . I was able to cobble together most of Ratliff's 'wasteful mastery' playlist, including songs by artists such as [Dean] Martin, Lil Wayne, Lou Reed, Fats Waller, Young Thug, and Nina Simone. It's a hoot, and it sold me on the book's central concept."

—Devin Leonard, *Bloomberg Businessweek*

"In this insightful guide to contemporary music appreciation, genre limitations are off the table. . . . Ratliff's scholarship shines; there's a lot to be said for a book on music appreciation that can draw apt parallels between DJ Screw and Bernstein's rendition of Mahler's ninth symphony."

—*Publishers Weekly*

"It's fascinating how Ratliff can bring a fresh ear to such familiar music. . . . [He] makes unlikely connections that will encourage music fans to listen beyond categorical distinctions and comfort zones."

—*Kirkus Reviews*

Every Song Ever

Twenty Ways to Listen in an Age of Musical Plenty

Every Song Ever

Ben Ratliff

Picador   Farrar, Straus and Giroux   New York

To Kate, Henry, and Toby
—who else?

picadorusa.com • picadorbookroom.tumblr.com
twitter.com/picadorusa • facebook.com/picadorusa

Picador® is a U.S. registered trademark and is used by Macmillan Publishing Group, LLC, under license from Pan Books Limited.

For book club information, please visit facebook.com/picadorbookclub or e-mail marketing@picadorusa.com.

Designed by Abby Kagan

The Library of Congress has cataloged the Farrar, Straus and Giroux edition as follows:

Names: Ratliff, Ben.
Title: Every song ever / Ben Ratliff.
Description: First edition. | New York : Farrar, Straus and Giroux, 2016. | Includes index.
Identifiers: LCCN 2015034664 | ISBN 9780374277901 (hardcover) | ISBN 9781429953597 (e-book)
Subjects: LCSH: Music appreciation. | Music—Psychological aspects.
Classification: LCC ML3838 .R29 2016 | DDC 781.1'7—dc23
LC record available at http://lccn.loc.gov/2015034664

Picador Paperback ISBN 978-1-250-11799-1

Our books may be purchased in bulk for promotional, educational, or business use. Please contact your local bookseller or the Macmillan Corporate and Premium Sales Department at 1-800-221-7945, extension 5442, or by e-mail at MacmillanSpecial Markets@macmillan.com.

First published by Farrar, Straus and Giroux

First Picador Edition: February 2017

10 9 8 7 6 5 4 3 2 1

Contents

Every Song Ever

Introduction

We are listening in the time of the cloud. First there was a person making up a song, as ritual or warning or memorial. Then there was a person singing an old song that someone had made up. Then there was music in the church and the concert hall and bar and bordello; then the wax cylinder, gramophone, radio, cassette, CD player, downloadable digital file. And then there was the cloud. Now we can hear nearly everything,* almost whenever, almost wherever, often for free: most of the history of Western music and a lot of the rest.

We know all that music is there. Some of us know, roughly, how to encounter a lot of it. But once we hear it, how can we allow ourselves to make sense of it? We could use new ways to find points of connection and intersection with all that inventory. We could use new features to listen for and new filters to listen through. Even better if those features

---

*Can we really hear nearly everything? No. There is much more to the history of music than what has been copyrighted, recorded, and negotiated for by media companies. And you should keep that in mind as you read this book. But the idea of "everything" is true enough for us to feel its truth. The amount is hard to quantify—a lot of music, in relation to what?—but its force is real. Even the most knowledgeable don't know it all, or even the full extent of it. We have reached the point that the Tao Te Ching, in Arthur Waley's translation, describes: "the further one travels / the less one knows."

and filters are generated more from the act of listening itself than from the vocabulary and grammar of the composer.

The most significant progress in the recent history of music has to do with listening. How we listen to music could be, for perhaps the first time in centuries, every bit as important to its history and evolution as what the composer intends when writing it.

By "how we listen to music" I am not referring to a change in our neural processing of music. (This is not a scientific book.) I mean a change in how we build a conscious framework or a rationale to listen to all kinds of music. Culture is built on ready availability, and we have suddenly switched from being a species that needed to recognize only a few kinds of songs—because only a few kinds were readily available to us, through the radio, or through record stores, if we were lucky enough to live near one—to a species with direct and instant access to hundreds of kinds, thousands of kinds, across culture and region and history. Listeners have become much more powerful. Perhaps we should use that power to learn how to listen to everything.

Here's an image from real life. A teenage boy, on a bus in the Bronx, in a puffer vest and bright kicks and a close haircut, just old enough to have figured out how to dress with authority, listening to a song by Jeremih, phone to ear. Maybe he bought the song; more likely he found a way to download it for free, or is streaming it from YouTube or Spotify. The song is about luxuriant sex, as are most songs by Jeremih. The teenager listens with near boredom and absolute confidence. The position of the phone in his palm, the angle of his hand and wrist, the focus of his eyes as he surrounds himself with the song's information—this is all part of his creativity. He is engaging, identifying with the song; he has a sense of dominion over the song and the medium. He can take that song or leave it. There are a million others like it. He's got the power. He's the great listener of now.

He can listen to more, or he can listen to less. He can hear a musician perform twenty times without paying admission or traveling any-where, through live streams on screens. If he finds his way to the right free software, he can time-stretch a song while keeping it at the same pitch, and turn its emotional experience upside-down, as has been done to records by Justin Bieber and to the Jackson 5. He can fuse elements of two different songs—say, a Biggie Smalls rap and a children's television-show theme—and can learn, when boomeranging it through social media, that a lot of people (mostly young people) really, really like stark musical juxtapositions.

In the store where he bought his sneakers he might have heard a digital playlist on shuffle, playing a Don Omar reggaeton track after a Latin freestyle hit from the 1980s. On the bus, he can stream the same five Drake mp3s from the cloud without owning anything he's hearing, or he can listen just as easily to recent field recordings of Saharan music, possibly made on a cell phone. At home, he can watch television shows that use recorded music pulled from any tradition of the last hundred years in order to give extra meaning to a scene or a character; if he likes what he hears, his cloud-based playlists might appear to follow no associative logic of sound or style. Later on, if he becomes more en-gaged with music, he can—let's say—train as a violist and feel moderately sure that he will work with electronic-music composers or singer-songwriters or Berklee-trained guitar improvisers or rappers from South Africa. He can walk out of whatever styles of music raised him, and into others as yet unknown to him, where he has complete access because listening gave it to him. He doesn't have to wait for music to define him. He can define it.

Music is everywhere. It has gained on us as our waking life turns into one long broadcast, for better and for worse—often for worse. But we have gained on it, too, learning how and when we want to absorb it. The unit of the album means increasingly little to us, and so the continent-sized ice floes of English-language culture that were Beatles and Michael Jackson records are melting into the water world of sound. (For efficiency we'll download just one song and ignore the other twelve, but we could likely have them all for free: we have a new assumption that music is ours to take, just as soon as it is ready to be sold to us.) We might get our cues about what to listen to from our Facebook feed, or from sources that use music as almost neutral content in a mediated environment—talent shows, talk radio, football-game ad spots. Background-music services have been vastly improved, thanks to the information yielded by our online listening activity. Pandora's so-called Genome recommendation model reminds us that there is more to be heard within a similar style, based on that style's small or large characteristics. Other sophisticated music-data algorithms, such as those created for Spotify and other clients by music-data companies like the Echo Nest, profile your taste in music as a condition related to who you are in general—where you live, how old you are, how you are likely to vote. With these advances we can essentially be fed our favorite meal repeatedly. We develop a relationship of trust with—what? Whom? A team of programmers? Our own tastes, whatever that means, translated into a data profile?

This all sounds very bad. It probably is very bad. Infinite access, unused or misused, can lead to an atrophy of the desire to seek out new songs ourselves, and a hardening of taste, such that all you want to do is confirm what you already know. But there is possibly something very good, too, about the constant broadcast and the powers of the shuffle and recommendation effects. There is a possibility that hearing so much music without specifically asking for it develops in the listener a fresh kind of aural perception, an ability to size up a song and contextualize it in a new or personal way, rather than immediately rejecting it based on an external idea of genre or style. It's what happens in the moment of contextualization that matters: what you can connect it to, how you make it relate to what you know.

The old way of "correct" listening involved more preconditioning. It meant not only knowing where a piece of music came from historically and nationally, but physically: an oboe sounded like an oboe. A celesta sounded like a celesta. A viola like a viola. These machines had right and wrong ways to strike the ear. One understood those sounds by imagining those instruments within an ensemble or orchestra arranged on stage and facing the audience. A certain language of rhythms and harmonies, signposts and cues, became consensual within a culture.

But since and after the 1970s—when studio recording suddenly advanced beyond the limitation of eight tracks, synthesizers and then samples became common, and various extremes of volume or experimentation in progressive rock and jazz and electronic music developed their own traditions in popular culture—the listening experience has been changing. You often don't know what you're hearing. Pierre Schaeffer, the French composer, saw that coming in the 1950s. "The lessons of the linguists must be born in mind," Schaeffer wrote, speaking of the failure of Western notation to encompass all music. "A foreign language cannot be reduced to the familiar patterns of our mother tongue. We have no doubt that other civilizations probably have other instruments and other ideas, a solfège of their own, perhaps more refined than ours."

And that's what listening can be today: an encounter with civilizations other than your own, perhaps on a daily or weekly basis, no matter who you are. Older listeners might feel it more intensely: having grown up with predigital sounds, some feel that nearly everything they hear through the channels of popular culture is strange or even unknowable. But even younger listeners feel something like this, too. Even if they've used Garageband, even if they've used digital editing programs to make a YouTube video, they may still be disoriented by the intensity, the sounds and swells and curves, of a Max Martin or Maybach Music or DJ Mustard production, or all that flows from those headwaters. Sounds are running ahead of our vocabularies for describing them. Oh, we have a general idea—those sounds come from digital sources—but perhaps we don't expect the frequencies of those sounds, or how they will be arranged.

The feelings of disorientation, of not knowing what process makes what sound, of not really understanding what "producers" do, are question marks now built into our hearing. We have not been thinking so much about the old definable coordinates. We have been thinking, when we hear something that is new to us, more about affect and magic. We are redefining our terms every time a new piece of music arises in the shuffle rotation, because there is a greater chance that we will be surprised by its juxtaposition with what came before, if only in volume: the very loud mastering of the Black Eyed Peas, let's say, coming after the dun-colored restraint of a Waylon Jennings record from the mid-'70s.

In many cases, having rapidly acquired a new kind of listening brain—a brain with unlimited access—we dig very deeply and very narrowly, creating bottomless comfort zones in what we have decided we like and trust. Or we shut down, threatened by the endless choice. The riches remain dumb unless we have an engaged relationship with them. Algorithms are listening to us. At the very least we should try to listen better than we are being listened to.

To a certain way of thinking, understanding Beethoven's or Bach's use of melody, harmony, rhythm, tone color, and compositional structure might have taught you how to listen well in 1939, when Aaron Copland published his popular book *What to Listen for in Music*. Copland called this the "sheerly musical plane" of listening—the state of being alive to what he called music's "actual musical material," "the principles of musical form." It was an ideal of listening according to an imagined sense of what the composer would have wanted you to understand. But Beethoven and Bach, even combined—and great as they still are— do not prepare or condition you for the range of music that in 2015 is already, or could easily be, part of your consciousness. It is up to you to come up with reasons for engaging as a listener that can encompass Beethoven and Bach as well as Beyoncé, Hank Williams, John Coltrane,

Drake, Björk, Arvo Pärt, Umm Kulthum, and the Beatles. They don't all come from one tradition, and their principles of form are different. They're not all standing on one sheerly musical plane.

Perhaps those reasons for engagement could be articulated in a language that isn't specifically musical, or identified with composers and players, as Copland would have wanted, but rather a language that refers to generalized human activity. Therefore, perhaps not "melody," "harmony," "rhythm," "sonata form," "oratorio." Perhaps, instead, repetition, or speed, or slowness, or density, or discrepancy, or stubbornness, or sadness. Intentionally, these are not musical terms per se. You know what repetition is even if you've never had the first thought about how a song is written. You know because you experience it in your average day or week. Why is it all right to categorize music this way? Because it has to be all right. Music and life are inseparable. Music is part of our physical and intellectual formation. Music moves: it can't do anything else. The same goes for us. Everything has a tone and a pitch, and rhythms—or pulses, at least—surround us. We build an autobiography and a self-image with music, and we know, even as we're building them, that they're going to change. Most human beings impose their wills on the world partly with and through music, even if they are not musicians. The way they hear—you can call it taste, if you want—is in how they move and work and dress and love.

Repetition, for instance: repetition in music works best when the quality of repeated tones and their patterning remind you of breathing or walking or running. Crucially, the effect of repetition depends not on one figure being repeated identically and unaccompanied, but on a relative change moving against a relative constant, which is really the key to life's riddle of time and gratification. Once you establish that, you can hear it in a piece of music by Rihanna and then make connections to other examples of musical repetition: James Brown, and Steve Reich, and Cortijo y su Combo. All those entities may belong to different radio or streaming-service playlists. But so what? When the first order of business is to sort music out by genre or structure or language—to determine whether a song is indie-folk or classical or R&B or whatever—that's a direct route to the bottomless comfort zone.

And so, back to the question. We can listen to nearly anything, at any time. How are we going to get to it? How are we going to access it, and how can we listen to it with purpose—meaning, how can we pay just enough attention to it so that it could change our lives? And again: How are we going to listen better than we are being listened to?

This book is a series of essays about different things to listen for in music, now that the circumstances have changed since Copland's time. Nobody can love everything, of course; the urgent thing, now that we have so much catching up to do, seems to be how to access a strategy of openness, a spirit of recognition. It means rolling the microscope back from issues of form and genre to find general associative qualities that have to do with the actual experience of listening, such that you might perform your own version of "If you like X, you'll like Y," in which X and Y may have been conceived centuries apart, for totally different audiences, and yet they're both in front of us, equally accessible. I am attempting to respond to a situation of total, overwhelming, glorious plenty.

This new kind of thinking about listening—if it is new—will be speculative and somewhat subjective. It uses "I," "we," and "you" in a generalized way. (Of course, the "we" might have a little more to do with me than you, and the "you" might also have little to do with you. It's a rhetorical conceit.) It talks about some very simple notions, such as repetition, and a few that are more abstract and intuitive, such as what I call "linking," and that might require a little more squinting and imagining on the part of the reader. Listening—reacting to music and putting yourself in its spaces—is an abstract and intuitive job.

But no reaction to music is universal. The old way, of learning to listen through the lessons and aims of the composers, could be speculative, too. The journalist and music-appreciation writer Henry Krehbiel, a democratizing force for general audiences around the end of the nineteenth and the beginning of the twentieth century, speculated all the time. In *How to Listen to Music: Hints and Suggestions to Untaught Lovers of the Art*, from 1897, he wrote statements such as "the lifeblood of music is melody," or "the vile, the ugly, the painful are not fit subjects for music." Some might only partially agree with him now. Some would say he was entirely wrong.

I am not going to give you an algorithm for finding new music to know and love. It's not my business to anticipate what you might like. I am suggesting a strategy of openness, and a spirit in which to hear things that may have been kept away from you. The suggestions I'm offering for how to hear are based on certain kinds of affinities between pieces of music. The affinities are not based in genre, because genre is a construct for the purpose of commerce, not pleasure, and ultimately for the purpose of listening to less. (I sometimes use words and phrases that have to do with formal structure and genre in this book, but where it is possible I try not to. Most of all, I am trying not to use those terms as boundaries or to confer value.) This book is about listening for pleasure, and about listening to more.

1. Let Me Concentrate!

〜〜〜〜〜〜 Repetition

When we talk about "repetition" in music, we don't mean one unchanging tone, or exact copy of a tone, over and over, without evolution. That doesn't give you any reason to keep listening.

Early on a recent morning, just after five, a car alarm lit up the atmosphere outside our window. It produced one continuous tone, for about thirty-five minutes. What a surprise, and then what a trial. It bore right into my hearing. I didn't think about the various overtones that made up the sound, as I do whenever I hear the distinct blasts of the commuter train whistle down by the river, because the alarm was unceasing, purely irritating.

Obviously there was no human hand behind the sound, pressing a button down for some sufficient length of time. But it soon became clear that there had been no human programming to *change* the sound, either. I didn't even momentarily consider that someone needed to know his car was being burgled. I thought: Someone needs to kill that car. And then give its owner a new alarm, one that uses repetition instead of an unchanging tone.

When and why do we use repetition in our own behavior? There is a bad sort of repetition we fall into, unknowingly. We use it when we're being greedy or punitive, self-absorbed or cruel. We might practice it in the form of repeated scolding, or silently trawling through all possibilities of personal failure, or checking e-mail every ninety seconds. It is compulsion. It happens whenever we tell ourselves we may get something new out of the process, even though we know we don't.

But there is also good repetition, perhaps more periodic than continuous, with longer or perhaps irregular breaks between the actions. This kind of repetition might suggest positive upkeep, or providing for others, or adding to an ongoing process: helping your child get ready for school, cleaning your car or bicycle, doing the shopping, exercising. Expressed in music, the stops between tones allow the listener to think about how to move forward.

In music there's imagined to be a general split between two orientations: variation and repetition. But it's not a pure split. They coexist in music, as they coexist in nature. Everything we tend to classify as "variation"—sonata form, symphony, jazz—includes repetition. And everything we tend to classify as "repetition"—minimalism, reggae, R&B, techno—includes variation. The best of what we call repetition in music, heard closely, is really the opposite of repetition: subtle differences, slowly shifting backgrounds, a change moving against a constant.

If all music is ritual—which it all is, in some form—then let's say that variation celebrates the proliferation of life; the theme that binds the variations together implies a unifying power, maybe even a theistic one. Repetition is a little more about music itself, and thus a little more about humankind alone.

Repetition is a smart psychological operation—a way to make you focus on all that is in fact nonrepetitive. The music seems to stay put, while you (or your perceptions) change. Then you stay put while it changes. It suggests infinity or eternity, basically. But only by distant representation. We couldn't have actual infinity or eternity in art. We would hate it.

Repetition often leads to length, to the expansion of an idea. The idea of dividing a recording into a "part one" and "part two," in order to accommodate and justify that expansion, had grown familiar by the late '60s. It began not as an aesthetic conceit but a necessity, when classical pieces were divided across sequential sides of 78 rpm records. In 1935, Duke Ellington imitated that convention with a curious, inward, lovely, thirteen-minute, four-sided piece, *Reminiscing in Tempo*: he was calling attention to the fact that he could write in long form as ably as many classical composers—and perhaps with more originality.

But gradually this convention of record-making became more of a response to the demands of the body. When people start dancing, a kind of ownership ritual takes over. They've marked out their own physical space: it now belongs to them. Likewise, they've started to take ownership of the music they're hearing. They don't want it to stop. After imitating other people for most of the day, or week, or year— their mothers or fathers or supervisors, their smarter or more beautiful acquaintances—finally they're playing themselves, in whatever form they want. They can be as free as they want, as elegant or debased as they want ("We're dancing like we're dumb-dumb-duh-duh-duh-dumb," sings Kesha in "We R Who We R").

There are few ecstatic rituals outside of churches and bedrooms. Dancing is one. Making records is not. Making records is pushing against a clock ticking counterclockwise. It's playing in front of people who are thinking primarily about when and how you will finish.

In 1937 Benny Goodman wrapped "Sing, Sing, Sing," a concerto for his drummer, Gene Krupa, around both sides of a 78, labeled "part 1" on side A and "part 2" on side B. Later, rhythm-and-blues musicians and producers, having inherited the youth audience for jazz, made the idea their own. In 1959, the Isley Brothers recorded "Shout," parts one and two. In 1964 they did it again with "Testify," parts one and two, a crazy party, high on its own momentum, full of impersonations—of Ray Charles, of Stevie Wonder, of James Brown—and powered with a sped-up version of the rhythm used by every Twist song in the world. In 1967 Lee Moses made "Bad Girl," parts one and two, jangly and tense with a habanera beat. There were many others.

Releasing a single this way was based on an actual need. The need was to stretch out, to go long. Everyone understands why musicians sometimes need to go long. Why do kids want to play outside until the moon comes up and they can't see the football anymore? Why do new lovers want to stay in bed all day? It's the act of recording, the force of the gate coming down, that doesn't make sense. So, a six-minute single: that's putting something in the wrong box. That's healthy.

Here was a mode of resistance disguised as gimmick. You hear side A and you know the song, but you worry there might be something hidden in side B. Sometimes it really was all one piece, unintelligible if you didn't hear the whole of it. Sometimes it really was graspable by listening to one side, and there was little more to it than length: expansion for its own sake. At what point can you assume that repetition only leads to more of the same, or that it won't lead you to a new perception of what you're hearing? It's a good question. These records toyed with that question.

"Ain't It Funky Now" (parts 1 and 2), not a particularly famous James Brown song but in my opinion one of the greatest recordings in the world, works like a container for the ideas about repetition and length that he and his band were playing with in 1969.

Let's assume that "repetitious" and "long" are not pejorative words in music. Repetition is a sign of health. Granted, it's also a sign of sickness. In fact, sometimes repetition is *totally sick*.

The 45 rpm single of "Ain't It Funky Now" advertised that the artist had something to say with a group, a collective process to work out in real time. It was proof, in case anyone didn't already know, that the JBs were important, best understood as a process and a movement of their times; that Brown's records weren't just three-minute confections over a factory band. It also worked as an advertisement for buying the LP at higher cost, because there you'd find the whole mesmerization intact, without the fading edit in the middle.

And it was a step closer to a representation of infinity.

In "Ain't It Funky Now," from the first seconds you hear tension and contradiction. The rhythm guitarist, Jimmy "Chank" Nolen—his nickname an imitation of his sound—strums a quiet, steady-lurking note making a wary ninth against the horns, which repeat their own melody, happy-major and staccato. But everyone in the band, from the beginning, plays softly, entering like the team of burglars penetrating the jewelry shop in the Jules Dassin movie *Rififi*. It's the opposite of something else Brown did well, the first chord as room-clearing explosion, as in "Papa's Got a Brand New Bag." Starting quiet generally means you might have a plan to stay quiet for a while, and thus raises an important question: What kind of game is that?

Then Brown does an amazing thing. (It might not have been amazing had you been there; it might have looked like nothing more than a jam session. But it is amazing when framed and reproduced.) He starts to talk, rhythmically, sometimes repeating himself, not really going anywhere, cycling through his catalog of phrases, as an improvising musician does, as a preacher does, as oral poets do. But the classical way of improvisers and oral poets is to use nubby stock phrases as signposts or ending places for long lines. He is using only the nubby phrases.

"Ain't it funky now," he repeats, as often as he likes, sometimes as a neutral marker in between the band's repetitions, and sometimes as an exclamation, centering your attention. "Heh," he says, making little touches to the big matrix of rhythm, like an extra drummer. "Huh-huh."

He plays a couple of short solos on the organ, warning beforehand that he's about to do so. They're unschooled and concise, blunt, unresolved; he grounds them in a limited vocabulary of licks and figures.

On a record, specifically on a record called something-or-other parts one and two—implying that there is something to be said here, work to be done—his act of casually taking inventory, checking in with his own tricks, takes on a different mystery. What's he up to? What's the point of this?

He is describing what he's about to do and what he wants the band to do in turn and keeps a running description of it, like a sports commentator. "A taste of organ," he notes, before and during his solos. He keeps punctuating with his voice as he plays: "Heh." "Huh." And then in a sudden, gruff command: "*Hit me!*"

A dynamic shift brings relief. The band breaks the pattern, switches the rhythm from 4/4 to 3/4, and blasts out three steps up a major scale; the drummer rolls twice, the band blasts out the same three steps down, then plays, all together, one of those "Papa's Got a Brand New Bag" chords, as if to say, "*and now . . .* " And now, what? Back to the usual: the soft, needling repetition you heard at the start, the major-minor friction, the spiel. What's he saying? He's describing what he hears and what he feels, but every line has its own emphatic rhythmic phrasing.

"Good God now," he says. "Heh." He further repeats the song's title, at regular intervals. He echoes the title of a Horace Silver song from some years previous: "Filthy . . . McNasty." He creates a surge of phonetic power with the phrase "preacher daughter." He makes sounds with his mouth open and with his mouth closed. He treats his musicians like a commanding officer, or a dominant lover, pinning them with his attention ("You. Yeah, you.") or asking them the same questions over and over again. To Jabo Starks, the drummer: "Do you like it?" "Sure is funky now," Starks responds. "Do you like it?" Brown presses. Four questions, four answers: yes, yes, yes, yes. At a point in Maceo Parker's saxophone solo, he lashes out, exercising his power. "Man, *quit that noise over there!*" He pauses. "Take it down!" Another pause, and then Brown says something beautiful, maybe the signal moment of the whole six-and-a-half-minute song: "*Let me concentrate!*"

All good repetition in music is embodied by that demand: let me concentrate. The musician earns your trust through some form of a question, a testing of boundaries and a half-turn away from the audience. Music is a game between performers and audiences, a loop in which performers hold the upper hand, then audiences, then performers again. The performers, however, have the home-court advantage. They always make the first move.

Music doesn't *have* to do anything, enlightened listeners like to say. Well, yes it does. It has to begin, and it has to end. And for a lot of people it has to be recognizable as music, at least in some context. Being recognizable as music usually means that it makes the listener feel one way or another, enlightened or soothed or nostalgic or turned up. For an "entertainer" to ask for his own space can seem out of line, a form of breaking the social contract, like a chef emerging from the kitchen after you've ordered to tell you that he feels like switching your dinner to something else.

Steve Reich, as a student, was fascinated by the importance of rhythmic repetition in Javanese and Ghanaian music. (He wasn't too invested in European music after the middle ages. "Frankly, my interest in Western music slacks off from Perotin onward," he told an interviewer, when he was thirty-five.) He'd also been studying at Mills College in San Francisco in the early 1960s, where, alongside Terry Riley, he was involved with the locus of early tape-experiment music, the San Francisco Tape Music Center. Those three elements—a love of repetitive rhythmic music, a disinterest in the classical tradition, and a curiosity about tape edits that could build staggered waves of repetitions—led him toward writing pieces that subtly changed as they obviously repeated. His art is the sleight of hand with which he masks the changes; the effect of the art is physical thrill.

Four Organs, from 1970, is one chord, essentially an E dominant eleventh, played by notes divided among four Farfisa electric organs, that gradually changes its emphasis, taking away its root note of E and moving toward an A. (Changing the implications of a chord through different voicings, until the chord might be unrecognizable as such out of context, is a common musical strategy.) Underneath the organs, maracas keep up a steady metronomic shake.

Over the fifteen minutes of the piece, you come to know the chord in many implications, just as you come to know the tense atmosphere of the James Brown song. But the chord is implied in staggered waves; it flickers. You're just about always hearing a note within it. But the greater part of it, the wholeness of it, appears unpredictably.

This aspect of *Four Organs*—its "repetition"—is like playing a peekaboo game with a child. You're going to do it over and over: that's the repetition. But you've got to keep changing the way you do it, otherwise he'll expect it and will not be surprised. And at some point in the game—it doesn't take very long to get there—you and the child understand each other: you know each other's reaction time, range of facial expressions, sense of humor, degree of patience.

Of course, there has been repetition and length in music forever, among friends or in situations that amount to ritual. But over the last sixty years audiences in more formal or isolated settings—in supper clubs, in theaters, in front of the television set, in the car—have grown sophisticated about elaborate repetition and transgressive length in art.

A lot of that change happened in New York. In the late 1950s John Coltrane and Sonny Rollins started to teach listeners that thirty-minute saxophone solos weren't only for dancers on a jump blues, but for sitting, absorbed-by-the-particulars kinds of audiences. Coltrane and Rollins—both in New York—and the composer La Monte Young, an Idaho-born jazz enthusiast studying in California, all started hearing Indian music between 1957 and 1961. (Ali Akbar Khan's *Music of India: Morning and Evening Ragas*, one of the earliest Indian classical-music recordings by a single artist to appear in the West, was released in 1955; Coltrane almost certainly was listening to *Religious Music of India*, released by Folkways in America in 1952.) Young wrote *Trio for Strings* in 1958, a piece that opens with a viola's a C-sharp drone held for three to four minutes before moving on. He relocated to New York in October 1960. Andy Warhol, who may or may not have been present at a performance of *Trio for Strings* in 1962, soon thereafter made *Sleep* and *Empire*, two long films, five and eight hours, that dealt almost exclusively with duration and the changing consciousness of the viewer.

Since then, the valuing of repetition for its own sake has become a shorthand sign of intelligence, not merely a show of avant-garde credentials. *Four Organs* was reviled at Carnegie Hall, in 1973. "The audience reacted as if red-hot needles were being inserted under fingernails," wrote Harold C. Schonberg in his *New York Times* review. Many listeners left. A few cheered. Schonberg disapproved yet hedged his bets: "At least there was some excitement in the hall, which is more than can be said when most avant-garde music is being played." But two weeks later, in a think piece about new composers, he put the knife in, turning what he saw as hippie condescension back on itself. "There is no 'content' in this kind of music," he wrote; "it is pure sound, and there is nothing to 'understand' in it." He continued: "Really it is 'art' for people who are afraid of 'art.' Or do not understand what art really is. Or who are too emotionally inhibited to want to share the intellectual processes of a real creator's mind. 'Four Organs' is baby stuff, written by an innocent for innocents."

But Chic's first single, "Everybody Dance"—a bubbling disco song with much ennobled innocence and much repetition—was, reportedly, loved in its first habitat: a Manhattan club called the Night Owl, where the disc jockey Robert Drake played its white-label prepressing, sometimes several times in a row, in the months before its release in 1978. Chic included the guitarist Nile Rodgers, an artistic descendant of Jimmy "Chank" Nolen; his scrubbing, scratching, trebly rhythms held together songs that sounded twice as good in their eight-minute-long, extended versions as they did in the three-minute radio edits that made them popular. (The formula was already there in the group preceding Chic, the Big Apple Band: surviving videos show grimy, graceful, deep-groove funk.) Rodgers and his songwriting partner in Chic, the bassist Bernard Edwards, would talk about what they called the "deep hidden meaning" of their songs, a notion they eventually called DHM. In interviews, he has spoken of DHMs for various songs having to do with current events: the state of the economy, or ongoing racial inequalities in America. Those are good answers for interviews, but I am convinced that they understood the creation and dismantling of the repetitive act as its own DHM.

As Harold Schonberg's words illustrate, in a formal context—of tradition, manners, or the academy—repetition, at least until recently, has not been all right: it has had associations with childishness, time-wasting, and primitivism. But in a context of play, repetition is and has always been very all right.

The animated television series *Family Guy* makes a lot of jokes around repetition. In one recurring joke, the main character, Peter Griffin, hurts his knee, by falling or being kicked. Reflexively, he says "Aah!" and sucks in air through his teeth. He does it again and again: "Aah!" *Sssuck.* "Aah!" *Sssuck.* "Aah!" *Sssuck.* By the third time, the viewer becomes aware that it will not be leading to something else—Peter rescued by a medic, Peter mocked as a wimp by a bypassing child, et cetera. It is a totally inside loop, something about how we react to pain, letting out serial cries in bursts, maybe soothing ourselves with our own repetition. It's about how strange it is to repeat an action and how easy it is to stop the flow of time. The sequence can go on for what feels like an indeterminate stretch. It is essentially the show's creator, Seth MacFarlane, saying, "Let me concentrate!" It is a kind of music.

We're familiar with the way standards are set by an individual performer, or by a group, or by a producer, or by a record label, or even, on rare occasions, by a consensually understood genre. But it is rare to find the title of a song acting as a guarantee that it will be good, or at least possible.

I know of six excellent songs called "Don't Stop the Music." Rihanna's, of course. Then: Yarbrough and Peoples. George Jones. Lionel Richie. Del McCoury. Playa, the Timbaland-produced boy group.

I have found more than forty songs called "Over and Over." Again, for a search conducted only by title, most of what turns up is better than good. Some concern themselves with God and the delicate operation of daily living (Vashawn Mitchell, Margaret Bell). Black Sabbath's speaks of persistent psychological pain; the MC5's, of the futility in war and policing. Most of the rest are "about" dancing, or attraction, or sex. But of course they are really about music: the repetitions. That is their Deep Hidden Meaning.

There are all the standards on the same subject: "Night and Day," "I Could Have Danced All Night." Jimmy McHugh's two great songs of compulsion: "Say It (Over and Over Again)" and "Can't Get Out of This Mood." Sammy Cahn and Jule Styne's "There Goes That Song Again," with its self-fulfilling lines:

> There goes that song again
> We used to call it our serenade
> We fell in love when we heard it played
> Over, and over, and over and over again.

And there's the thing I heard George Clinton say about halfway through a P-Funk concert: "We ain't going no-fuckin'-where."

DUKE ELLINGTON, *Reminiscing in Tempo*, 1935
KESHA, "We R Who We R," 2010
BENNY GOODMAN, "Sing, Sing, Sing," Parts 1 and 2, 1937
ISLEY BROTHERS, "Shout," Parts 1 and 2, 1959
ISLEY BROTHERS, "Testify," Parts 1 and 2, 1964
LEE MOSES, "Bad Girl," Parts 1 and 2, 1967
JAMES BROWN, "Ain't It Funky Now," Parts 1 and 2, 1969
STEVE REICH, *Four Organs*, 1970
ALI AKBAR KHAN, *Music of India: Morning and Evening Ragas*, Angel, 1955
VARIOUS ARTISTS, *Religious Music of India*, Folkways, 1952
CHIC, "Everybody Dance," 1978

2. Past Present Future

~~~~⩊⩊⩊⩊⩊⩊⩊~~~ Slowness

Recently I have been feeding songs into a depth machine: a digital conversion processor that uses an open-source audio editor to, at my settings, slow down the tempo by 18 to 25 percent. The point is to make the rhythm of a piece of music noticeably slower than a normative musician or group, perhaps under the watch of a normative producer, thinking of the normative tastes of a normative marketplace, would make it.

What comes out the other end is music made stronger by a more privileged relationship with the senses. What was stressed becomes harrowed. What was fresh becomes curdled. The best I've found so far: "Would Ya Would Ya Baby," by the Jackson 5, in which what was good-natured becomes menacing. Slowing a song down after the fact changes its overall design: some songs don't have it in them to grow longer again by half, and you find yourself wanting to turn it off after the first revealing minute. But that's all right. You've gotten to the center of it, you've seen its insides. And perhaps the song has seen yours. Slowness in music invites reciprocity: it makes the listener want to fill the spaces with his own content, whether that be associations or movement or emotional response.

Slowness in music can only be appreciated without recourse to the notion of progress. You have to disable your modernity to hear slowly, or formulate such a way of listening that anything ancient can be also modern, which is a healthy action, no matter when, where, or why.

Deliberate slowness has been a radical exception to a general rule of speed. In general, citizens of developed countries are expected to put on a mild hustle so as to distinguish ourselves from the ignobility of all the old slow processes: nature, animals, farming, smelling the air to read the weather patterns. In the nineteenth century, the initial development of the railroad and photography led to the proliferation of a cliché cribbed from Alexander Pope—the phrase "the annihilation of time and space." You didn't have to run to get somewhere fast, and you didn't have to travel somewhere to behold its image. Since then, speed has been imperative. Hearing music that pretends the passing of time isn't important, that there isn't a more efficient alternative, puts us back in the 1860s.

You can hear amazing examples of it in the last hundred years— Sarah Vaughan's "Lover Man" on *Swingin' Easy*, so slow that it seems like a boast, so barren that it's an abandoned continent, which she walks like the only woman alive; or the Flamingos' "I Only Have Eyes for You," viscid, amniotic; or "Zip-a-Dee Doo-Dah" by Bob B. Soxx and the Blue Jeans, tough, limping; or Marvin Gaye's "Inner City Blues (Make Me Wanna Holler)" or Earth's "Descent to the Zenith," or Shostakovich's String Quartet no. 15. These are all in some way acts of resistance, orchestrated protests during an extended period of industry.

Over the last few centuries, I can't think of an entire style or aesthetic movement in music favoring slowness for its own sake—and not as an interlude to set against faster tempos—until the 1990s. Suddenly in hip-hop there were new, knowing forms of the slow jam. Then tempos themselves led the way: there was west coast G-funk and Houston chopped-and-screwed; doom metal, come back since the late-'60s Black Sabbath days and puffed out, restylized; trip-hop and down-tempo electronic music; the return of Shirley Horn and Little Jimmy Scott, sepulchral jazz-ballad singers, specialized tastes who in their advanced years locked in with audiences for who they really were.

It all had to be a reaction—how could it not be? It might have been to the high beats-per-minute count of drum-and-bass and jungle, which can itself be understood as a response to the sudden overwhelming revolution of the Internet and e-mail: forces that stole into our lives so quickly, with so much eager acceptance, that we didn't notice how they'd formed our brains until ten years later. It could have been a reaction to fatalism and loss of faith, at least the kinds experienced in America: the terrors of crack and AIDS and of incarceration rates that multiplied by seven between the early '70s and late '90s, or the strength of marijuana, multiplied by three during the same period. In any case, slow music had new reasons and functions.

Like country music and the blues, chopped-and-screwed music came from the rural south. Before his family moved to Houston, DJ Screw grew up on farmland in Smithville, Texas, south of Austin. Possibly influenced by a local DJ, Darrell Scott, he became interested in remixing hip-hop tracks at slowed-down tempo, an easy way to create a signature. Soon he was making customized tapes for friends, and selling his newest tapes out of his house, at the rate of a thousand in a few hours. He became a filter, a customizer, for the most popular MCs in Houston. He began to see himself as a radio station. He agreed to make tapes without payment, advancing the cause of himself in particular and slowness in general. (On the documentary *DJ Screw, the Untold Story*, the rapper Z-Ro said, "Back then, Screw tapes was really like a promotional team without legs." The music didn't have legs either. It had cilia.)

What Screw did was to put an original aesthetic ahead of market considerations. He kept the tempos low and the swing high. There had already been easy-rolling G-funk from Los Angeles, and some fairly slow and distinct Texas rap, such as UGK's record *Too Hard to Swallow*. But Screw's versions, and the middling but consistent fidelity of his mix tapes, really found the beauty and identity in regional speech, the close-to-the-ground swerves of black southern sounds. ("Under my damn be-yud, man I'm flipping re-yud, if I get caught with keys I'm goin' Fey-ud.")

His "June 27" mixtape, from 1996, had an almost unbroken half-hour tag-team freestyle over a steady vamp. It sampled Kris Kross's "Da Streets Ain't Right" (originally 86 beats per minute), which accommodated a sample of Biggie Smalls rapping from "Warning" (originally a touch slower). The "June 27" rhythm took Kris Kross from 86 to around 69 beats per minute. That's a magic zone, a speed the listener can crawl into. Fourteen years later, Gayngs, the Minneapolis band, made a whole record at 69 beats per minute, in admitted homage to 10cc's "I'm Not in Love," which has approximately that tempo. It also evokes screw music to anyone who wants to hear that in it. Without realizing it, 69 or thereabouts was the tempo I found best suited to my Jackson 5 intervention.

"June 27" is not just a track; it's a principality. Its mayor is Big Moe, who sings near Barry White's register and respiratory timbre, endlessly repping for Third Ward Houston; he was the great phlegmatic advertisement for sizzurp, the codeine-based drink that eventually killed him. He manages the track, introducing each individual rapper: D-Mo, Key-C, Yungstar, Big Pokey, Kay-Luv, Haircut Joe. (Big Pokey is particularly fine, deep into his Biggie Smalls.) They each rap about money, women, drugs, and cars, with particular attention to "barre" (sizzurp), "embalming fluid" (liquid PCP), and wood-grain interior finishes.

DJ Screw tapped the spot where his own originality came out, and created a frame for hip-hop to go long and promise infinity. The rapping in "June 27" wasn't slowed in postproduction; he pushed the tempo of the beat low enough that it narcotized his MCs in real time. Naturally or not, he helped them to sound like they could regulate their flow forever, in one extended-mix track until doomsday, and he did what only the most knowing forces in music do: he used his hearing to make others' hearing change. In the only video of him mixing on turntables, the rhythm of his scratching and dropping with a record of Southside Playaz' "Swang Down" mimics Texas speech. He's in no hurry.

It is devastating music, scarily adrift. But a historical reality about Screw music intensified that impression. By the time that music had grown at all beyond local Houston precincts, DJ Screw was dead—he, too, from a codeine overdose. So to hear it as popular music was necessarily to hear it as a memorial. "Is the sound of Screw the sound of death?" the critic Jon Caramanica asked in 2002.

Is slow music in general a sound of dying? Is that why Leonard Bernstein's last go-round with the adagio of Mahler's Ninth, released in 1987, was the slowest he conducted? (Bernstein wrote that through composing the Ninth Symphony, Mahler saw "three kinds of death": his own, the death of tonality, and the death of "society, of our Faustian culture.")

It's astonishing, and kind of moving, that DJ Screw's advanced version of a slow temperament came out of such a young person. Usually it emerges from older composers, older performers, those who think and move more slowly. The conductor Sergiu Celibidache's versions of Bruckner—the Seventh Symphony, or even better the "Benedictus," from Bruckner's Mass in F Minor, sound like a screwed version of other conductors' versions of the "Benedictus." (Leon Botstein's or Philippe Herreweghe's, for instance.) What is he finding by making the piece move so slowly?

Celibidache believed that as music becomes more dense it should also become slower, so that the listener may be able to hear its constituent parts. He also believed that each place and moment for a musical event has its own individual tempo, and that a conductor, or a musician, should determine tempo last, upon arrival and final preparation. "Music is not a preservable object," he said in a documentary film. "If you just understand it, you are not part of it." I believe this is correct, to the extent that any statement about music in general—all music ever made, for any purpose—can be correct. In an interview, Daniel

Barenboim has told a story that Celibidache heard Furtwängler con-
duct Beethoven's Fifth Symphony many nights in a row, and finally
asked the older conductor how he determined the tempo. "Depending
on how it sounds," Furtwängler said—or at least this is how Celibidache, who studied Zen and knew the rhythm of a koan, filtered and
retold the answer. This is the point: every piece of music, for every individual person, has its own inner speed, depending on what that person
believes the music is meant to express.

Slowness can be the speed of taking life in thoroughly, without
missing the details. It can be the speed of having no other distractions.
And it can be the speed of summing up, of finding a way to see life in
the long view, perhaps all chapters at once, with motion decreasing
in order to be understood. Shostakovich's String Quartet no. 15 was
completed in 1974, a year before his death; every movement is marked
adagio, and his instruction to musicians was, "Play the first movement
so that flies drop dead in mid-air and the audience leaves the hall out of
sheer boredom." That's a great line: it suggests the old movie fantasy of
frozen time, or of the writer and composer Jonathan Kramer's notion
of "vertical time" in music: "a single present stretched out into enormous duration, a potentially infinite 'now' that nonetheless feels like
an instant." That's a great line, too, a provocation and a metaphor. It
describes a perception, from a single point within a single piece of music, of what has happened thus far, what is happening now, and what
will happen later, all at once.

That may sound idealized, but why not enlarge the frame even further? What if there were an experience of listening, perhaps brought on
by a certain kind of slowness or a certain quality of phrasing, in which
one could experience vertical time not only within the single piece,
but of lots of pieces—all that the listener knows, perhaps, from music's
past, present, and future?

At any rate, it's hard to imagine Shostakovich meant what he said.
A lot happens, in solo and ensemble passages, in the first movement of
his String Quartet no. 15, and even more in later movements. Plus, his

comment suggests philosophical implausibility, in the same way that you can't say "I am dying and I don't have the strength to go on" in a performative way.

Maybe we need understatement instead. Maybe we need slow funk. Is there anything more worthwhile, more worth slowing down for? Funk is already predicated on playing slower than the beat, and on hearing slower than the beat; slow funk goes further in the right direction. For dancing, it's the sound of respect, the sound of holding and waiting. It can take the form of a kind of power ballad—Chic's "At Last I Am Free"—or of a steady ongoing groove in various tempos, from (in order of increasing speed) the Ohio Players' "Heaven Must Be Like This" to the Isley Brothers' "Summer Breeze" to Grover Washington and Bill Withers's "Just the Two of Us." It is music that creates instant judgments of morality: people have been known to hear the foundational examples of slow funk and connote it with love and respect.

They do that not only because of the lyrics. They do that because the rhythm section in this music—particularly the bass parts, running along melodic counterlines, using the width or skinniness of a note as an important factor in the overall sound—is rooted and planned and balanced. It demands to be heard and understood and internalized. It reaches up from below, from the lower frequencies, and takes care to slow you down.

Great trust lives in and around slow music. Playing it involves trust that the listener will stay with you; listening to it requires trust that the music will take you somewhere worthwhile. Religion follows trust. Dadawah's album *Peace and Love*, from 1974, luxuriates in slowness: it is a developed version of nyabinghi, the ritual hand-drum and chanting music of Jamaican Rastafarianism.

Its music slowly unfolds with voices, lead guitar, congas, bass, and the most rudimentary drum-set detail—often just a clenched high-hat, played softly, and a kick drum. That it walks without rushing becomes its pride and its individuality, its core identity. There are few records in Western pop (sacred or no, perhaps we can include this, as a relative of reggae, within Western pop) as content to move in steps as wary as these. This assembly of players—you'd never call it a band, because the music is so much greater than the musicians themselves—does something strange with the ear and the memory: you never know where you are in the song because the music remains essentially the same, a firepit jam that earns its weird tempo. Its beat stays amazingly wide; all fall around it fearlessly, knowing they can't put a foot wrong.

Of course music in slow rhythm is different from the placement of slow or full-bodied notes over a more regular rhythm, as in Miles Davis or Chet Baker. And it's different again from music that seems to live outside of rhythm, that uses it deeply and then abandons it as it needs: Paul Bley and Keith Jarrett and Cecil Taylor and Sunn O))); powerful, mind-over-matter stuff. Andrew Hill's powerful dictum was "I look at melody as rhythm." If you accept that melody is rhythm, then you're acknowledging that a melody needs rhythm internally, to hold together, but doesn't need it externally, as a grid. And so: one is the other. A melody can stop and reconfigure, and suddenly the rhythm is broken, renounced. In general, going slow in music—whether continuously and consistently or not—is a suggestion that rhythm either doesn't matter or can become subsumed within something else, such as melody, or resonance, or sound.

Going slow is a fantastic way to bring on a kind of trance. Slow music enlarges the area of music. Think of music as a stretchable city grid. Easing back the tempo pulls cities into the lesser density of exurban sprawl and finally into spread-apart desert villages. Suddenly you need more memory to imprint the signposts. The canvas is bigger, the intent more mysterious.

I am listening now to Sleep's album *Dopesmoker*. It's one track that lasts about an hour and three minutes, and stays in one key, mostly in one chord. The control is fantastic; the music takes root in the chest and the memory.

A riff is exposed and evolved. At 15 minutes, space clears for a guitar solo. At 19 comes a pause. At 38 and 50, more solos. Various simple passages—riffs, or orderings of riffs—are repeated so many times that you wonder at the containing logic. Was it graphed and charted? It must have been, and yet it seems nearly ritual, something done without their having written a single note.

How are you supposed to listen to this vast track, whose changes are so negligible on the small levels but so important on the bigger levels? You do your best. You bring the sound within yourself: it is grooving, organic, churning, basically one long body function—but you can't bring the structure within yourself. You can embody it, but not contain it. You have to disable the capturing part of your mind. What a perfect band name, Sleep. The music pushes you toward it. It won't let you see it clearly, alertly, structure-mindedly. It keeps walking forward on its scripted marathon trail of spiritual dumbness. A friend saw Sleep once. The music pushed him down, blacked him out. He fell asleep in the rear corner of the hall. The theater's custodial crew woke him up a while after the audience had left the building. "What's *wrong* with you, man?" they asked.

The singer in Sleep is not its guitarist, Matt Pike, but its bass player, Al Cisneros, and that is appropriate for music with such resonance. He sings in monotone chants, similar to what the guitar plays; his own bass playing is full, melodic, curious, ornamental, and an enveloping force. The band is a trio of rock, paper, scissors. The drums are the rock. The guitar, abrading and toothy, is the scissors. The bass is the paper. What a physical pull this music has—a downward pull. Slow and low. Never forget that this is finally us, it seems to say. Our general hominid origins but us *now*, too: a stock state of being, a basic starter set of instinct and heartbeat and self-protective impulse.

Years ago, in the mid-'90s, a brilliant and contrarian friend, J. D. King, wrote a short story called "Like a 45 on 33." Then, inspired by the story, he made cassettes of various songs, which he recorded to tape at improperly slow speed. It worked. What worked? *So much*. It was as if hidden powers seeped out of the songs, as cooking bones in liquid brings out the marrow, making the animal transform after its death. It's a process that brings the essence to the surface. There's always a second song within the first song. Slow tempos can reveal it, especially with a steady and formal dance beat. These are some examples of what I mean:

Satie Slowly, by the pianist Philip Corner, in which the pianist argues, through decelerated versions, that Satie's simplicity was not a flaw but a test of how strong a "simple" composition really can be.

"Donna," by Ritchie Valens: the Del-Fi 45 rpm single taken down to 33⅓. Oh, the original's soulful, if a little abstracted. Ritchie Valens is singing apostrophically to a woman; he has no plan, and feels romantic about that. ("Darling, now that you're gone, I don't know what I'll do," he sighs, contented in his misery.) But here a different emotion emerges. Even as slow as 50 beats per minute, the triplet rhythm remains acceptable, but Valens seems as if he's fighting to sing, as if there is something at stake, a catatonia to overcome. The downbeats land over the place; there's always a bass note when the drummer lodges his thuds into the song, but their precise point of contact keeps shifting; this is something you can hear more closely at slower speed. And Valens loses himself in his ballad, gives himself to it. Music at best, and like this, is an act of generosity.

"Funnel of Love," by Wanda Jackson, again slowed down from 45 to 33. (Thanks to the late DJ Todd Butler and the blog of the radio station WFMU, where I came across it in transformed state.) A minor-key curiosity by a rockabilly singer. The action is in the pinched, excitable, bad-baby bark of her opening lines: "There I go, fallin' down-down-down." A slower speed and lower pitch makes it the song of an aggrieved man, or an old male goat. The slowed-down version went up on WFMU's blog in April 2009. Five years later a variation of this became part of the soundtrack for Jim Jarmusch's film *Only Lovers Left*

Alive, in which two stylish vampires are portrayed as devotees of extremely slow music.

"Would Ya Would Ya Baby," by the Jackson 5, digitally lowered by 25 percent in tempo but not in pitch. A fuzz-funk, solid-groove Detroit song becomes New Orleans wormwood, in the process of moving it from 105 to 75 beats per minute.

William Basinski's *The Disintegration Loops*: slowed-down and repeated portions of Muzak tapes, pushed by the composer until they attain eerie beauty.

"Are You Sincere," by Pete Drake, the Smash 45 played at 33: an Andy Williams waltz-ballad covered slowly with voice-box steel guitar, like a wah-wah effect that forms words.

The collected works of Robert Johnson. A persistent rumor holds that Robert Johnson's recordings were sped up when pressed to the 78 rpm records. It has been convincingly argued, particularly by Elijah Wald, that this mistake in the transfer would have been unlikely. But there is a reason the rumor stays with us: slower tempos make the songs sound good. In its best-known mastering, Johnson's handling of rhythm, his dragging and syncopation, his filling of spaces and making them as long as he likes, sounds extraordinary, and not freakish: this is all part of why he's famous. But "Terraplane Blues," 15 percent slower than normal, makes those living rhythms feel even more alive, and his mournful voice more mournful.

In 2013 I reviewed a concert involving the electric guitarist Loren Connors, who plays slowly: each note is its own world, its own idea. I like what he does, but I don't understand it: it's too thin-toned and slow for me, so slow and in its own moment all the time that it seems to undervalue larger form. I wrote that he sounded as if he might lose his way. Connors responded on his Facebook page:

> I like to think about slowness. The same kind of thing was said about
> Billie Holiday, Lester Young, Miles Davis, Chet Baker, and on and on.

The truth here lies in the fact that a person ages internally. The fast-paced, technically strong youthfulness gives way to a deeper concern. Look at Beethoven's last quartets, op. 131 and others. Look at Chopin's last nocturnes. And other great composers. They all offer us their slower, deeper sound in their final days. Like Ebenezer's spirits, the spirit of Music past and Music present and even Music future is gonna haunt you. It sure will. And when you do get older, if it's truth you're after, you play like the man or woman that you've grown to become and you leave all the youthful techniques behind. At 63, I play like the man I've become, not the boy I once was.

JACKSON 5, "Would Ya Would Ya Baby," 1972

SARAH VAUGHAN, "Lover Man," from *Swingin' Easy*, 1957

FLAMINGOS, "I Only Have Eyes for You," 1959

BOB B. SOXX AND THE BLUE JEANS, "Zip-a-Dee Doo-Dah," 1962

MARVIN GAYE, "Inner City Blues (Make Me Wanna Holler)," 1971

EARTH, "Descent to the Zenith," from *Angels of Darkness, Demons of Light*, 2011

UGK, *Too Hard to Swallow*, 1992

BRUCKNER, Symphony No. 7, Sergiu Celibidache, Münchner Philharmoniker, 1994

BRUCKNER, Mass in F Minor, Sergiu Celibidache, Münchner Philharmoniker, 1990

DMITRI SHOSTAKOVICH, String Quartet no. 15, Borodin String Quartet, 1978

CHIC, "At Last I Am Free," 1978

OHIO PLAYERS, "Heaven Must Be Like This," from *Skin Tight*, 1974

ISLEY BROTHERS, "Summer Breeze," 1974

GROVER WASHINGTON, JR., and BILL WITHERS, "Just the Two of Us," 1981

DADAWAH, "Know How You Stand," from *Peace and Love*, 1974

SLEEP, *Dopesmoker*, recorded 1996, 2003 version, Tee Pee

PHILIP CORNER, *Satie Slowly*, 2014

RITCHIE VALENS, "Donna," 1958

WANDA JACKSON, "Funnel of Love," 1961

WILLIAM BASINSKI, *The Disintegration Loops*, 2002–2003

PETE DRAKE, "Are You Sincere," 1964

ROBERT JOHNSON, 1936–1937 sessions

3. Draft Me!

I f you are thinking of Bud Powell, you may be thinking of someone playing the piano fast. In his case the fast playing isn't antiseptic, streamlined, surgical, the sort of thing that makes you question the point. We can find plenty of examples of that, in which a technique seems to have been developed especially for the purpose of making fast playing nearly flawless. No: Powell played fast with great effort and emphasis, making the rhythmic lines supple and meaningful, and struggling to maintain his chosen speed.

Listen to "Salt Peanuts," recorded live at Birdland in March 1953, with Charles Mingus on bass and Roy Haynes on drums (about 360 beats per minute). Powell was playing in the brisk, jagged spirit of his time, generally, and his reputation, specifically.

Speed, in a tradition that goes back to the virtuosi of the eighteenth century—the Italians Niccolò Paganini and Muzio Clementi, the Austrians Carl Czerny and Franz Liszt—is superficially synonymous with charisma, though it is perhaps the most workmanlike element of the Romantic classical tradition in performance. Playing a great many notes with individual definition is an action tied to negative associations: competition, the limitations of the body, physical pain, and the risk of being dismissed for soullessness. The duel between Mozart and Clementi in 1781—Clementi played his showy, stultifyingly

mathematical Keyboard Sonata in B-flat Major—resulted in Mozart
writing to his father that Clementi had no taste or feeling. "A mere
mechanicus," he sniffed. It can be hard to listen to the end of Liszt's
Hungarian Rhapsody no. 6, as played authoritatively by Martha Argerich, without wondering whether the hundreds of octaves hammered
so quickly and mechanically in her right hand might cause tendon
damage. (And also without reflexively wondering whether anybody
can do it *faster* than she can, and wondering to what end it is all for.) In
any case, Kenneth Hamilton, in *The Cambridge Companion to the Piano*, sets the high era of Romantic pianism between the musical duel of
Franz Liszt and Sigismond Thalberg in Paris in 1837 and the death of
the virtuoso Ignacy Jan Paderewski in 1941—the year that Bud Powell,
at seventeen, started playing gigs at Monroe's Uptown House in Harlem.

Speed is a by-product of a time when soloists began to travel and perform more widely—when managers and audiences agreed that they
generated something of value beyond mere faithfulness to the written
score. But speed often becomes an aesthetic problem. If you're really
able to use it, you may have to be willing to work as an advertisement
for the precise discipline or genre or composer you are playing. You
have a gift, but the gift has you. You're special, but expendable.

If you were a jazz musician in 1953 wanting to play a song fast,
faster than usual, faster than expected or needed or even wanted, "Salt
Peanuts" was the one. It was the symbol of straight stunting, aggressive
showboating. Normally the drummer Roy Haynes found self-possessed
funk in everything at any tempo, and made velocity irrelevant. But
here even he is racing. Charles Mingus rarely sounded self-possessed
above medium tempos; the speed of this performance brought out his
aggression.

From Powell, what you hear is a quiet introduction, followed by the
beginning of the first set of "answers" to the melody's "question": the
repeated octave jump. Then the race begins. He's playing long lines

ending with a single abrupt unresolved note, the slanted autograph of bebop. The band flows, but not peacefully. The second half of the song is entirely a Roy Haynes solo, and it restores order; within himself, Haynes can maintain the speed. Then Powell returns: again, the sound of gnashing gears, a small motor quickly getting hotter than it should, a bit of danger.

They're hanging on. Can you hang on? The experience of hearing music like this involves questioning whether it's worth it, or whether you're up to the task. How much information can you process? What do you want out of music? Why are you here? Do you actually *hear* music that goes by this quickly? Really, how many people do?

Powell's language in his two solo choruses, after the thirty-second mark, is volcanic, and full of licks. When musicians play very quickly, their brains tend to function more automatically; they need to play a lot of notes to get the point of their aptitude across, and so you hear an abundance of phrases that run easily under the fingers. You can be impressed by Powell's adherence to the song's built-in turns when played at that speed, but not much is surprising in Powell's solo choruses except the improvisation at their beginnings and ends.

Perhaps there are more details that can't be heard. At a certain point, as a listener, you just don't know. You give up. And what have you gained? A statistic: the fact that you heard Bud Powell play "Salt Peanuts" faster than you thought it could be played. It makes a good remark: "Have you heard Bud Powell playing 'Salt Peanuts' at Birdland in 1953?" Maybe the answer will be yes; probably no. And then an evaluation, which is probably of no consequence; what matters is only that someone has done it.

Outside of art we hurry for two reasons: either to reach a place by an appointed time, to make up for time that has been misspent, and thereby to please others; or to save time, to get ahead of schedule, because we would like to do something else afterward to please ourselves. In a musical performance neither of those situations applies. One could say that Bud Powell is hurrying because he has to meet the drummer at the other side of a four-bar phrase, but this is his group—he sets the tempo—and, anyway, aren't the three people in this group all functioning together? Aren't they looking at one another and jointly managing their time, to some extent? Especially in a live performance— which this is—where do they have to go? What's their hurry?

Speed has no practical purpose in music. It doesn't inherently increase or enhance the feeling of the notes themselves, or the listener's physical pleasure. Speed is to be considered separately from music. Speed in music is like a sweater on a dog: mostly for show. It increases tension, and its death-ride futility can feel attractive. It represents a tacit contract between the player and the listener: we're in this together, and it might come to no good. I'm going to tighten my grip, and so are you. It doesn't elicit: it forces, always, and in its very best instances it can force counterintuitive feelings, feelings of humanness and frailty.

During Roy Haynes's solo in "Salt Peanuts," he changes rhythmic ideas every few bars: syncopated patterns, cymbal workouts, echoes of the song's melody. From 2:52 to 2:56, he plays something vaguely like a blast beat—a pattern of alternating and extremely fast hits on snare and tom, in unbroken stretches of sixteenth notes. (In punk and metal it has often been played without alternation—snare and high-hat and bass drum all together on every sixteenth note.)

The blast beat doesn't swing. It is a pure unit of speed, unmoored from context or reason. It sounds like a human trying to be a stuck machine, a damaged mechanicus. Why did blast beats flourish around the mid-1980s, in hardcore and death metal? Perhaps because they had a contemporary point of reference. They were like the sound of a defective or damaged compact disc in one of the early players, a bodiless slice of digital information on jammed repeat. Blast beats are frustrating and not lovely—you almost try not to hear them, you almost try to push them away—but they matter. They stay with you.

The first time I heard a blast beat as such—the basis of an entire song, not just a four-second sequence in a solo—was in 1984, at CBGB in New York, as played by the hardcore punk band Dirty Rotten Imbeciles, or D.R.I. I remember that concert, because I remember the feeling of frozenness, not knowing how to respond; it was the musicians one-upping the audience, in a "you asked for it" kind of way. (That concert was recorded, and you can now ascertain that "Draft Me" ran at around 360 bpm, like "Salt Peanuts.") It's one thing to play fast at jazz-club dynamics; it's another to play fast and loudly. We all recognized that we wanted it. It was the logical extension of the speed and concision that already made our music exciting: pushing it as fast as it could physically go.

"Draft Me" was 23 seconds long, and not the shortest song they played that day. It revolved entirely around the singer and the drummer. The logo of the band was a dancer in mid-skank, positioned like a speed skater in action, torso bent down and forward. It also looked like a young man sprinting. The drummer and singer made the armature of the sprinting man. The bassist and guitarist were merely trying to dress him as he ran. Naturally, the singer and the drummer were brothers—Kurt and Eric Brecht, from Houston.

Hardcore punk in the '80s was a late extension of of neatly moralizing, late-'50s-to-early-'60s-style radical social-science doomsday tracts, based on bomb paranoia and conspiracy theories: monolithic thoughts of the company man, the military-industrial complex, the power elite, when it was still clear to politicized artists who was us and who was them. It is based on the thought that something is being done to us against our will, and we'd better trace the torture, mimic it, throw it back at the torturers, enact it on ourselves as inside-out protest.

It is the sound of lack of control or oppressive control, and nothing in between. A part of listening to D.R.I. is understanding the strange and natural discrepancy among the instruments working at that speed, the impossibility of truly coordinated motion, and the physical feeling that impossibility gives you, as if you're being pulled in different directions on each limb. There is a humanness and practicality in recognizing that tension. But what's under the music is enraged and futile irony: Kurt Brecht is demanding to be "a trooper in the world police." He repeats the title phrase like a tic, making it jump right out of the song, listening to his brother for cues in the rush of it. And your listening body responds as if under siege: panic, catatonia. Futility isn't just expressed by the variable speed; it's built into the foundation of the music.

One of the great documents of straining to keep tempos is Jerry Lee Lewis's *Live at the Star Club, Hamburg*, recorded in 1964. The house band at the Star Club at the time was the Nashville Teens, from Surrey, England. They worked as pickups that night for Lewis, who was traveling as a one-piece to save money on the downward slope of his success, as did Chuck Berry, as did Bo Diddley. But the crowds at the Star Club weren't over him yet; it was a place where early rock and roll still had value.

The Star Club recording starts fast, with "Mean Woman Blues," and gets faster, into "High School Confidential." On the studio record of that song, released six years earlier, the speed stays at about 180 beats per minute: fast enough. In Hamburg, it starts at about 205 and climbs, slowly, steadily, up to about 215. Why not as fast as D.R.I.? Couldn't he take it?

It wouldn't have suited his rhythmic temperament, or the distinguishing marks of the music he identified with. D.R.I. hammers out two-beat hardcore. Jerry Lee Lewis is a boogie-woogie player, and needs to feel the two and four.

Like nearly every popular musician before the 1980s, Jerry Lee Lewis played for dancers, which means he played for sex. His syncopated four-beat rhythm worked with your body, gave it time to swing from one place to another. Sex is the opposite of futility, and this version of

"High School Confidential" works at the outer edges of what's possible when you are still interested in responding with your body in more than one movement—the swing, the rock and the roll. It is just below the level of incoherence or machinism.

Speed in music doesn't have a wide emotional range. Usually a listener perceives it as power or energy. But sometimes—rarely—extreme speed can be disciplined into pathos. There is an instructive difference between two versions of Scarlatti's Harpsichord Sonata in B minor, K. 27, by the Italian pianist Arturo Benedetti Michelangeli and by the Russian Mikhail Pletnev. Pletnev's is full of emotion, making its tempos undulate like a wave; the first of its many retards arrives three seconds into the piece. And the second time the opening seven-note theme is introduced, it sounds like Pletnev is considering the phrase anew, hesitating microscopically before the final note. It is collected and full; it is presentably beautiful.

Michelangeli's is unusually fast and tight, and slightly crazy. It alerts you of its intention to blaze from the very beginning, with instant momentum, but no annunciatory accenting, almost as if it's appearing edgelessly in the air, a sudden floating fact. And there is something withdrawn and sad about its excellence. It is *too* fast, after all. It doesn't need to be so fast. This isn't allegro, as the piece is marked; it's presto. There is something inhuman about it, something of the "mechanicus." It's a suicide mission. Of course it is accomplished, and indicative of great labor. But even in its relative quiet it has a hysterical edge.

Fast tempos have gone through several cycles in hip-hop—as novelty, as partial evidence of skill, and finally as hardened style, speed for its own sake. Tech N9ne and Machine Gun Kelly, for example, fall into their favored rhythmic patterns, determined to be faster than anyone else; they seem to rev high naturally, and they seem to be competing for dominance. (A situation in which the record, meaning the disc, becomes the record, meaning the certificate of achievement.) Busta Rhymes and Ludacris have flow and lilt, but they can be single-minded and ultimately narrow.

Big Boi and Andre 3000, from Outkast, made speed seem most natural and important to rapping. By the mid-1990s, they rhymed fast when they didn't need to, and didn't when perhaps they did; they swung their triplets expressively, as few but southern rappers could at the time.

By their second album, *ATLiens*, they were disobeying the rhythmic lines of the song, and drawing close to the microphone, so that they could be fast without shouting, without sounding strained or effortful. Sometimes they sang right through their speed; in "Da Art of Storytellin' (Part 1)," on *Aquemini*, they let the contours of the narrative lead their flow. By the time of *Stankonia*, in 2000, Outkast was doing so much with hip-hop—stretching out its tracks, using outdated beats and stabs with light and brilliant live bass playing, mixing it with psychedelic rock and P-Funk chants and high-speed European club music and sophisticated, outrageous humor—that it could use speed however it wanted. Speed was no longer evidence of greatness. It was just one strategy in a wide spectrum, with nothing crucial riding on it. That was when they made their fastest song, "B.O.B."—their most impressive display of speed, and perhaps their least imaginatively delivered.

Speed is a noticeable event, something we want to replay for our friends; we recognize it implicitly as a form of athletics, and also as currency in the economy of impressing others. Also, in recorded music, unlike loudness, with its mechanical limits, or sadness, with its subjectivity, or any of the other qualities that we're considering in this book, speed can *actually be measured*, via the metrics of beats per minute.

Does it matter how fast or how slow something is in beats per minute? Has it ever? Andre 3000 isn't as fast as Machine Gun Kelly, yet he's a better fast rapper. Happy hardcore techno, categorically speaking— there isn't much music that can be written about categorically with quite so much ease—is faster than D.J. Funk's bootyhouse or D.J.

Assault's ghettotech, but it has less texture and expression and traction. It erases its own body as it moves along.

Speed is connected to body, to impulsive feelings and the short game. It's best heard as an expression of joy, and best played when it seems to have no practical purpose: when it is not expressly to be understood as a method for proving great musicianship, or bettering someone else's record.

BUD POWELL, "Salt Peanuts," from *Birdland 1953*, ESP-Disk

FRANZ LISZT, Hungarian Rhapsody no. 6, Martha Argerich, 1966 studio video, YouTube

D.R.I., "Draft Me," from *Live at CBGB's 1984*

JERRY LEE LEWIS, "High School Confidential," from *Live at the Star Club, Hamburg*, 1964

DOMENICO SCARLATTI, Sonata in B Minor, K. 27, Arturo Benedetti Michelangeli, 1962 video, YouTube

DOMENICO SCARLATTI, Sonata in B Minor, K. 27, Mikhail Pletnev, from *Keyboard Sonatas*, 2001

OUTKAST, "Da Art of Storytellin' (Part 1)," 1999

OUTKAST, "B.O.B.," 2000

4. What If We Both Should Want More?

-------Transmission

There's a thing some singers do: they go transparent in their voices. They seem to become the property of other forces. When they sing it's as if they're ventriloquists, with some clear distinction between themselves and those forces. (If we were talking in religious terms, we'd say between themselves and their faiths.) They minimize themselves; not worried about outcome, they represent the forces in a pure state. They seem released from anxiety.

I am listening to John Lennon sing "Julia." He seems to be conscious of how very little matters except the essential things. He sings that half of what he says is meaningless, but he sings the line clearly, as if he's intending it as a gift or a direct message. He's giving what he's got, to whomever he meant it for—his mother, his girlfriend, a fusion of the two. And he is understating what he has to give, using his humility, real or simulated. The verses are absolute simplicity: the vocal line stays on one note until he arrives at the name of the woman he's singing to, which he respects, in a secular kind of way, with a four-note phrase: V-iii-ii-I in a D-major scale. He is having less humble, more complicated thoughts in other darker places in the song, but he will not project this onto Julia. He will sing her name with a more neutral respect.

It's all in the tone, isn't it? Tone doesn't demonstrably exist in composed notes. It exists only in played ones. It's the most human part of music, the carrier of emotion. A sequence of notes, or a combination of top line and moving harmony, is just an enactment of musical relationships. Here, even Lennon's acoustic guitar isn't full of tone—it's just soft Travis picking, a method, a strategy. But he puts great attention into the tone in his voice. He is being clear and sensitive toward the song; he is singing a hymn and giving it away.

Can you point at an emotion in music, and claim it as a function or property of the music itself, rather than of what the listener brings to it?

I say yes. It's a yes followed by some small print.

There exists an old debate, especially in the classical-music world, between so-called formalists and expressionists (or autonomists and heteronomists). Formalists believe that music, in and of itself, means nothing, or has nothing to do with the world of emotions; it is the result of a composer bringing his tools and craft to neutral material (tones, chords, rhythms, textures) and creating something formally pleasing to the ear. Eduard Hanslick, the Prague-born music critic who moved to Vienna in 1846 and became possibly the world's first significant music-appreciation writer—the precursor of Krehbiel and Copland and possibly this book, too—is understood as the king formalist. His long essay "On the Musically Beautiful," originally published in 1854, set out his terms. Any strong theory demands a countertheory, and Richard Wagner took a kind of counterposition, arguing for "the sublime" as an animating force in great music—originating in feelings, in spirits, in people and history.

Hanslick characterized the problem that he saw around him: the idea that whatever transports the listener in a beautiful harmony or melody "would be not these [i.e., the harmony or melody] in themselves but what they signify: the whisperings of amorousness, the violence of conflict." He allowed that all the duped listeners around him were partially right. "Whispering? Yes, but not the yearning of love. Violence?

Of course, but certainly not the conflict. Music can, in fact, whisper, rage, and rustle. But love and anger occur only within our hearts."

That's a restrictive thought, but he had a further idea, much less restrictive, almost liberatory. Music can mimic the *motion* of feelings, he wrote. That's all, and that's a lot, and perhaps that's enough. "It can reproduce the motion of a physical process according to the prevailing momentum: fast, slow, strong, weak, rising, falling . . . It can depict not love but only such motion as can occur in connection with love or any other affect, which however is merely incidental to that affect." If we are to allow that music is primarily motion, and if we are to allow that there is some kind of motion in feelings—a waxing and waning of states of mind—then, okay, he allowed: there's your connection. (About a hundred years later, in the book *Feeling and Form*, Suzanne Langer would build on this notion, writing that music imitated not feeling itself but *forms* of feeling: "forms of growth and attenuation, flowing and stowing, conflict and resolution, speed, arrest, terrific excitement, calm, or subtle activation and dreamy lapses.")

Hanslick's essay appeals to the skeptical mind. He rephrased his assertion, turning it around, drawing it over and over again from different angles. "It goes without saying," he supposed, "that instrumental music cannot represent the ideas of love, anger, fear, because between those ideas and beautiful combinations of musical tones there exists no necessary connection."

But a great work of criticism—and "On the Musically Beautiful" is a great work of criticism—is very often a kind of memoir, consciously or not. It seems clear that Hanslick had the critic's problem of prescriptively worrying for the greater good, and the future good. He didn't want music to live or die by the extent to which it represented emotion. He didn't want it to be judged according to how well it represented, say, remorse, or ambition, or piety. He saw the fascination around Wagner, and around Liszt's tone poems, and worried that heteronomism might poison music or bring the whole enterprise down. He couldn't let go. But by adding that extra clause—about how music may mimic the motion of a feeling—he almost contradicted himself, or showed what he really felt.

There is an aspect of Hanslick's essay that either discredits or ignores the way most people enjoy music and make it part of their lives. His worry made him a literalist. He disagreed vehemently with the notion that there was an exclusive relationship between a certain tone and a certain feeling, and he was probably right to do so. But how many people truly feel that there is one?

For instance, in a typical 12-bar blues, just before the I chord shifts to the IV chord, I experience the dominant seventh before the shift as a kind of a private slang from musician to listener, keeping him on the hook—something like "'Naw mean?" And I experience it this way pretty often. But I would never claim either that this harmonic movement always has that emotional meaning, or that it has it for everyone, or that it has it to the exclusion of any other meanings. Who would? Some kind of maniac. Hanslick might have seen a lot of maniacs around him, of a kind particular to the world of European classical music, because that world has long been concerned with what the composer allows, and with fixed standards of construction and execution.

There is a more tempered version of the formalist argument, expressed by the pianist and writer Charles Rosen, which holds that emotion is definitely expressed through music, but not through a universally applicable secret code. As he put it in *Music and Sentiment*:

> Most discussions of musical sentiment that I have ever seen seek to
> establish such a code, a symbolic system, even a relatively esoteric one
> with which listeners in the past were supposed to become acquainted.
> Indeed, in learning a language we are expected to learn to recognize
> the traditional meanings of a great many words. However, the trouble
> is that music is essentially a poor system of communication, precisely

because it has a rather weak and ill-defined vocabulary, although a very rich and powerful grammar and syntax.

Which is to say: music coheres and resolves according to lots of intrinsic rules—so many that we tend to call it a "language." But natural languages—excluding languages of math or computer coding, for example—typically have many specific words to point toward specific commonplace ideas. This language doesn't, or at least resists being used quite in that way.

Still, how often do we hear any music without at least *a little* bit of context to clue us into the notion that we are hearing music that has something to do with, say, love, virtue, or immortality? It is a basic measure of emotional intelligence to be able to read those symbols, either from the music itself alone, or with—as is usually the case now—some kind of chatter around it, a bit of myth or notoriety or a story told skillfully by a publicist. (Even a lie can become the truth.) We read the symbols and the lore and then listen through the filter of those readings. We ascribe love, virtue, or immortality on the music; it is part of the creative process of listening, whether we're doing it aesthetically or pathologically or in between. And then through our hearings we add a layer of meaning to the music, which eventually finds its way back to the composer or maker of the music, who can either accept or reject that meaning.

It doesn't matter so much what the music is thematically "about," in a program notes or *VH1 Storytellers* kind of way. It probably matters more what the musician is about. Hanslick had a good point when he wrote that Beethoven's "Egmont" overture could just as well be called "William Tell" or "Jeanne d'Arc." But because the piece is so Beethovenian, so full of his own strategies and determinist magic, we hear it as part of the story of Beethoven's own creativity.

Despite the weakness of music's universal vocabulary, there are some elements of the vocabulary we agree on, at least within individual cultures. We need to attach emotional descriptions to music in order to contain it, fix it, tag it, draw its boundaries, know what use it has, and remember how to find it.

But there is an extreme form of emotion in music that transcends specific moods. I'll call it a state of transmission. There are stories of Sufi masters, with divine agency, who use their powers of intent to send energy forth to their students. Students or seekers can feel the power of transmission by seeking to let go of their own existence and perceive the essence of their god. Receiving transmission (or *tawajjuh*) in the Sufi tradition has been compared to falling into a sea—a pleasant form of drowning, all-consuming, all-immersing. It is two things at once: a state of pious selflessness and a beaming forward; the musician's simultaneous connection to eternity or inevitability—as exemplified by a sound only he can make—and to the listener.

If Hanslick was suspicious that the listener could be moved by a single emotion, he has his analogue in devout Sufis, who deny that an ecstatic reaction at a Sama—a "musical ceremony for the attainment of a sense of union with Allah," as Judith Becker puts it—is caused directly by music. Devout Sufis trace that reaction back to two sources. One is *kaif*, a kind of prereaction, a secular appraisal of the music's delivery that perhaps conditions them for the more important process, which is *hal*, the trance state, the letting go of self and communion with Allah.

I'm suspicious, too. I don't think there is a specific sound of religious ecstasy in music. There are *conventions* in religious music— upward modulations, the Amen cadence, and so forth. But we're not talking about that. We're talking about trust in redemption, absolute confidence in the benefits of generosity, of willingness to get beyond earthly desires. We're talking about when a musician makes herself very small in relation to a force that guides her, and then directly transmits the force of that trust to the listener. That transmission is a motion. The musician gives with transmission, the listener receives with transmission.

When you have a great gift in music and set a great amount of energy toward maintaining and developing it—when you have dedicated your life to an idea of excellence and then self-preservation—then you are practicing a form of transmission every time you play. Making music eventually becomes a higher devotion to an unstable process—and what is that if not transmission? The only signs that you are doing it well are two simultaneous connections—to the essence of your own sound and to the consciousness of the listener.

The bass-baritone singer Andy Bey, since he entered his mid-'50s, has sounded like a transmitter in nearly everything he's done. He tends toward two kinds of songs: those he has written, with dark warnings and clear morals, like a Bhagavad Gita, and standards about abiding love—"You'd Be So Nice to Come Home To," "I've Got a Crush on You," "The Other Half of Me." He is best without anyone else, accompanying himself on piano. And there is a sense of a higher calling in his slow-moving love songs. They are rituals. The standards he chooses contain common ideas about love, but he universalizes them further by slowing them down and spreading them out and reducing their sense of flirtation and nicety: every jitter, every affectation, every joke, out, out, out. You will take him plain, as his own sound, or not at all, and he ends up giving you more than you came for.

Giving more than you need to is an act of transmission. So is exposing doubt through music, admitting that we don't have the answers or the plan, writing words embodying that lack of a plan, singing in a way that embodies those words.

The Maze song "The Morning After" is like that: a song about a moral compromise—infidelity—that asks all the right questions, over slow, reduced funk, bringing none of the answers. The singer is Frankie Beverly, and his character seems to be speaking his mind something like twenty minutes after sex with someone who is not his wife. He sings about the satisfaction of the moment, but in terms of ongoing need. He also sings about the danger of the moment, and the people he could be hurting, and even of the people she could be hurting. He is having large thoughts that keep getting larger; the consequences multiply as he sings. He is judging whether the night has been worth it, because he fears an investment of emotion in someone who might quickly lose interest in him, or vice versa. That and the opposite, too: What if neither of them can control their desire in any acceptable way? What if a good thing can only become a bad thing? He asks, reasonably, "How will we know what we are doing / And what if we both should want more?"

Beverly is singing without recourse to answers. It's a song of love and pain but also of supplication, appeal to whatever stands above reason: those answers have to come from somewhere. And the music holds steady, with damped guitar strings, synthesizers set to flute sounds, twinkling percussion, and slow-walking tempo. There is nothing heroic in here—just worry, and commercialized sounds of thinking and feeling.

But the implication in the rhythm and structure of the song is that it could go on for much longer. What Beverly's character needs, and what the band as its own character needs, is to stay in place, to have more of now. He's not a supercharismatic or virtuosic singer, but he is one who appeals to a listener's sense of the daily rounds, and he goes deep. ("Quiet storm," they used to call this kind of music, the phrase itself suggesting transmission or surrender: an extreme action that refuses to become self-aggrandizing.)

Toward the end of the song he builds up to a single note and holds it for a long, long time—seventeen seconds. As long as we stay here we won't get hurt. This is the motion of not wanting to move. It portrays a gigantic and undefined need—to express gratefulness, to serve one's craft, to make time stop. It's a need that lives apart from worldly concerns, and doesn't have a timetable or an endgame.

So we don't need to know what the words to a song mean, or out of what tradition the song is operating, to adduce a spirit of devotion. We come to a slow minimalist acoustic-guitar song with words coming out in careful, continuous long exhalations; or a song with highly variable (but generally glacial) tempo, and subtle harmonic shifts sung in a deep, settled voice; or a slow jam with twinkling percussion—and we know. It is respectfully acknowledging something more powerful and mysterious than the singer himself.

And what about the Sufi tradition? I am listening to, and watching, a 1983 live recording of "Haq Ali Ali Moula Ali," by the great Sufi singer Nusrat Fateh Ali Khan, a song that became his first hit in the late 1970s. It is dedicated to Ali, son-in-law of Muhammad and said to be the originator of the Sufi orders. In this performance, as in others, the song moves slowly and heavily, prefaced by a long introduction with harmonium, hand drums and handclaps, which builds the tempo and the groove and the tonality until it becomes ironclad. At that point, Nusrat steps in. Swiftly, he transmits. His long tones envelop the ongoing drone note, fuse with it, punch through to your hearing: an act of forceful attention, attention manifested through sound.

The song works both all at once and spread over time. It makes its case in the opening minutes but digs in further through gradual changes in tempo, the shifting around of the lead vocal among the group of singers around Nusrat, the attainment of greater and greater speed, the provoking of ecstatic dancing, and finally the steering to a landing spot. Like "Julia," its lyrics—translated at Nusrat.info—are about saying a name to connect with a spirit force. He's making the connection in real time; he's accessing a kind of power, and giving it to the listener.

> Chant this
> As this is the name that is true.
> This is the name that removes suffering
> [And] the auspiciousness of this name opened the secrets of
>   being.

THE BEATLES, "Julia," 1968

ANDY BEY, "You'd Be So Nice to Come Home To," from *Ballads, Blues & Bey*, 1996

ANDY BEY, "The Other Half of Me," from *Chillin' with Andy Bey*, 2012

MAZE, "The Morning After," 1993

NUSRAT FATEH ALI KHAN, "Haq Ali Ali Moula Ali," UK performance, 1983, from YouTube

5. We Don't Need No Music

~~~~~~~~~~~~~ Quiet/Silence/Intimacy

One morning a couple of years ago I was listening to Morton Feldman's magnificent solo piano piece *For Bunita Marcus*. It's a very easy piece to listen to.

It is also very quiet. Sometimes it doesn't seem like it's pitched expressly at the ears of its audience; it sounds like something you might be overhearing. The sustain pedal stays down throughout, the slow but irregularly played notes linger for up to twenty seconds, and the tones overlap. In accordance with the score, the pianist—here it was Hildegard Kleeb—repeats patterns but then changes them, so that you are allowed to let go of the memory track and just listen, without proprietary feelings. But perhaps despite yourself you start to capture certain phrases; it becomes hard *not* to capture them, as you start grasping the form and spirit of the piece. As they enter your bank, they take you by surprise. You may wonder whether you have the right to keep them.

Anyway, something funny happened around the middle of the piece. During a repeated two-note pattern—if this were another composer you might say an obsessively repeated two-note pattern, but nothing about this piece is obsessive at all—an E flat two octaves above middle C was repeatedly sounded, or touched. (It's a quiet piece to begin with, but Kleeb plays the notes as an eater, holding a fork, breaks the surface of a buttery cake—with the understanding of it as a luxury.)

The E flat sounded very close—much less than a half step, maybe ten cents off, or a tenth of a half-step—to a warning tone made outside my window by a backhoe, moving dirt in the park. Both sounds shared a quiet presence in the room, and they were at odds. You had to accept the clash—what was the choice, elect to listen only to the backhoe?— but there was a prize in the acceptance of it. In other words, not asking what the clash is doing to you, but what it's doing for you.

You can practice radical acceptance if you're sick and your body is acting beyond your control, and you can practice it as a listener, when sounds act upon your consciousness. Quiet music, in the best cases, heightens the possibility of acceptance. It puts you on heightened watch.

The story of the twentieth century was not only the story of large-scale outward movements—telecommunication, postcolonial liberation, and total war. It was also, among other things, the story of self-absorption and self-guided spirituality, the time of going way inside for one's own gain. It produced the apotheosis of the small self, the heroics of aloneness, and the rules of self-sacrificing art. Look at all the lights voluntarily put under bushels in the middle of the century, as rhythm and blues was giving way to rock and roll, as Little Richard and Johnny "Guitar" Watson were excellently, outwardly straining and gnashing:

In 1952, John Cage writes and performs "4'33"," and Nat King Cole's trio creates an instrumental version of "I Surrender, Dear."

In 1954, Chet Baker records "I Fall in Love Too Easily," the Modern Jazz Quartet records "Django," and Dorival Caymmi records *Canções Praieiras*, for voice and guitar alone.

In 1955, Frank Sinatra records *In the Wee Small Hours*.

In 1956, Chris Connor records *He Loves Me, He Loves Me Not*, and João Gilberto discovers his sound while practicing in his sister's bathroom.

All of this musical activity is to some degree about the performer's privacy. It treads an ambiguous line between breaking a contract with the audience and giving them more of what they want. None of it, however, comes across as a quiet that's meant to comfort, or to appease, or to curry favor. False intimacy is the kind that tries to elicit a fixed reaction, that is calculated to comfort in order to score a point. Real intimacy has no stated goal. It is full of its own untranslatable reasons.

In art, the confident gesture, loud or quiet, is of highest importance; perhaps it's even all there is. By extension, the acknowledgment of the human behind it—the actual machinations of the finger, limb, or torso making the art—is secondary, if relevant at all. The dance critic Arlene Croce had an excellent way of putting this: "the arabesque is real, the leg is not."

She was talking about ballet as a code of "signs and designs." Let's talk about music that way, at least for now: as a code of signs and designs. Music is artifice. It is an organization of sound that expresses feeling. The effect of the minor chord, on its own or in its context, is real; the position of the hand is not. The stab and decay of the amplified note is real; the input and output levels are not. The vibrato is real; the larynx is not.

Quietness is the idea of open space, an idea that can mean very little or very much. (Of course there is no open space, really, in earthbound life; there is always something there.) Open space, whether in a park or a poem or a song, is first an element of design. And then it is a sign, a signifier or a symbol.

You realize the power of a short silence when you hear it in a song. You realize it in the middle of Metallica's "All Nightmare Long," in the tiny break before James Hetfield takes a gulp of air to keep singing, or at the end of the Beatles' "A Day in the Life," after the strings finish rising and before the final chord; and all through Aaliyah's "Are You That Somebody," where the silences seem to swing because they last a fraction of a second too long, or Erik Satie's Sarabande no. 1, where the one-beat rests break up the waltz time so often that you might never experience the song as being in three, or in any particular rhythm at all. Silence confounds, enriches, clarifies.

In some sense the listener is always playing along with the music herself, in her own way, through the nervous system or the memory, if she's heard it before. By that formulation, quiet—which, when taken to extreme, is silence—represents the opportunity for the listener to breathe, whereas all other musical matter requires that you hold your breath, concentrate, navigate. Quiet represents letting go, not hanging on; respite, not responsibility. You can hear it, but you're hearing metaphor as much as you're hearing content.

Used with a little rigor or aggression, the conscious production of less sound or no sound can turn the act of listening upside down. It means that the listener can be listening to, and responding to, absences. Feldman's *For Bunita Marcus* consists as much of decaying notes as sounded notes. Some works by Bernhard Günter or Ryoji Ikeda or Michael Pisaro can strike the ear as silence, even though something musical is usually happening and usually continuously: a small, sustained tone or disturbance, either digital or field-recorded. (John Cage's "4'33"" is silence, if we define silence in music as the musician not producing sound from his instrument. That does not mean it isn't also music, in terms of a composition, performance, and listening experience Cage intended to be musical.)

Those are extremes. There is another form of quiet, however—one that is not represented by actual silence. It is intimacy, which isn't measured in seconds, but in minutes.

João Gilberto's bossa nova recordings—all of them, but particularly some of those heard on his album *João Gilberto*, recorded in New York in 1973 and often called the "White Album"—are among the great examples of what we're talking about.

Intimacy is a reaction against all that is normal and acceptable in performance. It is the rhetoric of speaking only to one person, as opposed to thousands. At its best it commands by withdrawing: it can sound selfish, a self-limiting of potential. Or it can sound generous, as the most or best that a shy person can muster. It draws you inside the performer's instrument or respiratory system.

After his first few years in music as a member of the young vocal group Garotos da Lua, João Gilberto retreated from performing in 1956, staying with his sister in the Brazilian state of Minas Gerais, reportedly singing and playing guitar in her small tiled bathroom, where he found the acoustics perfect.

Seventeen years later he was living in New York, a Bahian speaking halting English. He was living in his own head, and might have wanted to get his listeners in there, too: there is a sense in his music from that time that he is playing for an audience in his memory or in a fantasized, ideal projection. Two songs on the "White Album" make the case especially well for the force of intimacy, and both are about home: "Falsa Baiana," an old samba by Geraldo Pereira, and a version of Gilberto Gil's "Eu Vim da Bahia." He's changed the tone of the humor in them. They were once social songs. Now they're cloistered, but they still have the samba rhythm inside them: Gilberto could create it alone. Great musicians can contain within themselves the force of more than one person.

He made the album in New York with one other musician, Sonny Carr, a drummer who worked on Wall Street by day and would obey Gilberto's edict of playing with only brushes on a clenched high-hat cymbal. It was engineered by Wendy Carlos, the organist of *Switched-On Bach* and creator of the soundtrack to *A Clockwork Orange*, who positioned a microphone close to Gilberto's mouth and changed the way he sounded on record. It is the closest to the ideal of his performances, and it set a model for how his voice would later be recorded. It is here that you can really consider what singing in a small tiled space may have done for him.

It also went far beyond the intimacy of his first recordings in the late 1950s, the recordings said to have modernized Brazilian music.

That modernizing, curiously, seemed to go against the idea of music as a social force, as a shared popular culture of samba-canção and bolero. It was the acknowledgment of a Brazil without crowds. Gilberto arrived with the sound of a new masculinity, an extreme vulnerability. It came from a number of sources, mostly American: Frank Sinatra's "In the Wee Small Hours of the Morning"; the Brazilian singer Dick Farney; the controlled, continuous tones of Frank Rosolino's trombone in the Tommy Dorsey band; and probably Chet Baker, who made his first vocal recordings in 1954. For all that, it was barely emotional. Its undulations were minuscule. The voice had no vibrato, and it came from the head; the "ba-dum-ba-baw" he sings toward the end of "Falsa Baiana" sounds like the thinnest muted brass.

Gilberto disappears at the end of some words, sometimes making you feel like he's removing himself to his ideal place. The word "cantar" in "Eu Vim da Bahia" ends with a small, aspirated "ah"; it is the uncommon example of an aspirated "ah" in popular music that isn't sexual. He demands, consistently, almost sullenly, that you listen hard to him: true passive aggression, a quality not abundantly found in pop until the 1980s.

If you understand music as free enterprise, which is how most people in America have understood it since the decline of the piano in the living room—the mid-1970s, pretty much—then the spectrum of quietness, intimacy, and silence in music might seem a form of selfishness or self-sabotage. It is not wanting to be heard, or only wanting to be heard on your own terms.

But if you listen another way, the quiet impulse might be a populist idea. It might reach more people. It is an expression of civility. It is not trying to interrupt or drown out anything else. It allows for the rest of life to be heard.

And it connects to a much greater pool of history and human expression. Quiet music intimates daily living as much as performance and stage business. It doesn't favor the biggest, proudest expression as the only true form of music-making; it is trying to transform what is casual, unspoken, or overlooked into a musical vocabulary. It is building a continuity between rest and motion, thought and articulation, sleep and alertness; it's always doing the work of connecting audiences, musicians, and people, rather than holding one above the others.

You don't just hear the glory of the quiet impulse in music that is downcast or meditative by definition—ballads or bossa nova or slow jams or folk song. You hear it nearly all the time in some musicians: Curtis Mayfield and Arthur Russell and the Modern Jazz Quartet, for example.

Curtis Mayfield was one of the great quiet music-makers of the twentieth century, and one of the wisest: intimate even when protesting racism over funk beats. The sound of his guitar and his voice seemed to work in alignment. He played a Telecaster without a pick, finding a trebly and clear guitar tone with subtle ministrations of the wah-wah pedal to offset the respirated breathiness of his voice. He raised his boy tenor up to a calm falsetto; he figured out ways to be prophetic while delivering a relatively low signal. He let you hear the dip and catch in his voice in the important vowels of each line, where many other singers might sing full and steadily. At best his art was like highly melodic talking heard at close range. And it was civil. He created space in his music so that others could be heard. There is always a sense that he has secured your permission and will play by the rules.

One of his most representative moments comes on the record *Curtis/Live!* in 1971, in "Mighty Mighty (Spade and Whitey)." After the second chorus the volume cuts and he sings about how everyone bleeds like everyone else: he's making connections. "Can I get a bit deeper?" he asks, then suggests that all human life comes from the same source. He declares that he is black and proud: he's telling you what he is and how he feels about it. He's rallying your conscience, but politely: he is preparing you to be a little bit surprised by a sudden change in volume or attack, or by an idea that takes some self-possession to express in public. But when he sings the slogan, he doesn't sing any louder than before. And after the next chorus and a bass solo comes an amazing sequence. The whole band cuts out, except for the conga player. "We don't need no music," Mayfield sings; "we got conga"—which makes sense if you are defining "music" as something made by a band. A few lines later he goes deeper, as he warned you he would. "We don't need no music," he repeats. "We got soul."

Nearly any given piece of music proceeds along the supposition that it is crucial. It is fighting to be heard, or conforming to a recognizable design, or otherwise validating its claim on your time, earning its length or seriousness or volume level. Curtis Mayfield, in his lyrics and in his sound, was willing to admit that "music" is secondary to greater things, that it can make room for better versions of the truth. In doing so, he gave it away genuinely. As a friend once pointed out to me while listening to this song, how many other musicians can suggest without rancor or resentment that we don't need music? John Cage couldn't. He disliked the accepted idea of music. He wrote in his book *M*: "Music ('good music') excludes the stranger, establishes the government, renders the composer deaf."

This is not primarily a book about words and music. It mostly considers words as components or representations of sound. But in this case, the words and the sound are expressing the same thing.

Arthur Russell was a soft-voiced singer, too. He created the music for his album *World of Echo*, according to his biographer Tim Lawrence, through midnight sessions, on "pretty much every full moon between 1983 and 1986." Like Curtis Mayfield, he had a sentient relationship with his instrument, which was the cello; he used digital effects on it to make it echo and bulk and warp and flood your hearing—to make it replicate things that the voice can do. He was making music connect, spreading it out, rendering his music simple and complicated at the same time, perhaps confounding its purpose a little bit in the service of magic.

He hesitated before finishing anything he'd started; he recorded much of *World of Echo* in the control room and edited with a razor on the fly, erasing bits of tape and recording over them, fully aware of the possibility of bleed-through, which shows up on the final product. He liked the word "liquefy": he wrote of "liquefying a 'raw material' where concert music and popular song can crisscross." And in his song "I Take This Time," he sang the lines "You made a sound that's in an early state / That liquefies inside before it's old, before its energy is over."

In most of his music, but especially in *World of Echo*, he made supremely quiet, intimate music. The entire thing sounds made for himself alone, like sections of an endless rehearsal tape; the songs seem to make reference to a single other person, as if they're to be heard only by that single other person, and received as a gift. (How many times he uses "you" intimately in the lyrics: "A kid like you could never understand"; "I'm putting everything around you / Over by you"; "I'm hiding your present from you"; "Although you're coming back, it's our last night together.")

You can draw a connection between it and João Gilberto; I do. But there's no evidence that Russell himself, who died in 1992, ever thought about João Gilberto. Bossa nova is a form, and he wasn't following any particular form. More generally, *World of Echo* is not "quiet music" per se. He was trying to bring out music that was not preconstructed, that sat liquefied inside him, through the possibilities of amplified cello and through using the tonal possibilities of his voice, singing from the nose and back of the head, slurring words, improvising, changing his accents and melodies, extending sections at will so that there was no such thing as verse or bridge or chorus.

And the Modern Jazz Quartet: What were they up to with their strangely soft dynamic range, with all those brushed drums, their own law of

seldom rising above a given volume level even as they played fairly intense music? They seemed to flout obvious logic, obvious laws of taste
and expression. The drummer Connie Kay could sustain interest even
playing a rhythm nearly unchanged for ten minutes, with scant off-beat
accents as weak as raindrops. John Lewis seemed always to be playing
less on the piano than he was expected to. "Bluesology," on the album
Fontessa, is as true and deep a blues as there is in African-American
music, but it feels as if it's made of thin china. Milt Jackson plays the
vibraphone without sustain, and Lewis's solo overlaps sneakingly with
his; counterintuitively, it contains very little. Toward the end of it, where
we might expect signs of a climax, he's playing the piano in parallel
figures with three fingers: two in the left, one in the right. It is willful,
surprising, and almost unnecessary: the definition of a successful gift.

MORTON FELDMAN, *For Bunita Marcus*, Hildegard Kleeb, 1990

JOHN CAGE, "4'33"," 1952

NAT KING COLE, "I Surrender, Dear," 1952

CHET BAKER, "I Fall in Love Too Easily," 1954

MODERN JAZZ QUARTET, "Django," 1954

DORIVAL CAYMMI, *Canções Praieiras*, 1954

FRANK SINATRA, *In the Wee Small Hours*, 1955

CHRIS CONNOR, *He Loves Me, He Loves Me Not*, 1956

METALLICA, "All Nightmare Long," 2008

THE BEATLES, "A Day in the Life," 1967

AALIYAH, "Are You That Somebody," 1998

ERIK SATIE, Sarabande no. 1, Aldo Ciccolini, Angel, 1968

JOÃO GILBERTO, *João Gilberto*, 1973

CURTIS MAYFIELD, "Mighty Mighty (Spade and Whitey)," from
   Curtis/Live!, 1971

ARTHUR RUSSELL, *World of Echo*, 1986

MODERN JAZZ QUARTET, "Bluesology," from *Fontessa*, 1956

6. Church Bell Tone

~~~~~~~~~~Stubbornness and the Single Note

Thelonious Monk recorded his song "Thelonious" in October 1947. In the second chorus of his piano solo, he plays one note, over and over—a B flat in the octave above middle C—for eight bars, about a quarter of the whole chorus.

It makes a lot of sense to do what he did, when and where in the song he did it, both on the small scale and the big scale. In the written theme, the horn players change chords on every other beat. But the lead voice, Monk's piano, mostly plays a B flat (and occasionally an A). It's an example of taking the idea of the drone or pedal point, which usually lies beneath a piece of music, and putting it on top instead. (Much the same thing happens in a more universally recognized song: Antônio Carlos Jobim's "Samba de Uma Nota Só," best recorded by João Gilberto.)

You notice that he called the piece "Thelonious." Let's suppose that he meant it as a tone poem about himself. It could describe the world around him changing rapidly, while he stays the same, a single note, over and over. A monotone. There is more in the rest of the solo—a building on those rapid chord changes, partly in a stride rhythm, and several of his typically short and abrupt downward runs in the right hand. But those eight bars are the soul of the song. They come right in the middle and they ground the operation. That series of the same note over and over acknowledges melody and rhythm and harmony. Just one note, the truest and realest thing he had as a musician. With two notes you have structure, and you are already graduating into the possibility that someone else has played that structure before. But with a single note you have authenticity, because nobody else has played the single note exactly the same way.

I once heard a music student ask Sonny Rollins about what constitutes a good practice session. He said that if a musician can make one note, one sound, that he feels happy with, it's a good practice session. A sense of relief broke upon the room. Rollins was not saying that a musician doesn't need to build a composition, or learn flexibility, or learn various harmonic strategies for soloing—none of that. He was only saying that music made by a person with an instrument boils down to a single tone. What's more important?

For the listener, the eight-bar stretch of the "Thelonious" solo stretches just past the point of being comfortable. At the beginning of those eight bars you think, "There's a man who knows what he wants." Then you think, "There's a man who believes in keeping it simple." By about the sixth bar you reach the third stage: *He's making a point. What is it? What am I missing?*

"Thelonious" isn't a piece of music about repetition. This is an outbreak of stubbornness within a greater whole. What Monk did in "Thelonious" doesn't only have to do with time; it has to do with tone. For the listener, it has to do with getting all the way around a single note, hearing it in full, understanding how it feeds into the changing mesh of the music and temporarily opens it up. He is getting up and walking around that note, just as he would get up from the piano during gigs and turn in circles. He is sounding it until it finds accordance with his own interior rhythms and he is playing it both as musician and listener. He is getting comfortable and encouraging his own creativity, and doing so with a magic indifference to what you might want from him. ("It is said of a very great Persian poet who was also a mystic," wrote the Sufi master Hazrat Inayat Khan, "that when he got into a certain mood he used to make circles around a pillar that stood in the middle of his house. He then began to speak. People would write down what he said, and it would be perfect poetry.")

Why is it that so many performances that lean on a single note sound important, sound like events? For example:

- Neil Young's guitar solo in "Cinnamon Girl": a restatement of the phrasing in the lyrics, through one note. "I could be happy the rest of my life," he sings: with his hands he demonstrates exactly what he means.
- John Lewis's piano solo in the Modern Jazz Quartet's "Pyramid," both on the studio album *Pyramid* and the live *Blues at Carnegie Hall*: a blues in E that becomes a tinkling obsession with the E of the octave above middle C.
- Johnny Ramone's guitar solo in the Ramones' "I Wanna Be Sedated": only eighth notes; a pretty good imitation of the states of nonthinking and nonfeeling.
- Roddy Frame's guitar solo in Aztec Camera's "Oblivious," which with its plateauing on E and then running scales up to the note makes it seem the son of Arsenio Rodríguez's tres solo in "Cero Guapos en Yateras" (1946), or something like it.
- Drake, rapping in the middle of "Furthest Thing": "You know I stay reminiscin' and makeup sex is tradition but you been missing girl and you . . ." In one breath, all around B.
- Johnny "Guitar" Watson's guitar solo halfway through Floyd Dixon's "Let's Go Smitty": a chorus of jump-blues springboarding on G.
- Illinois Jacquet's long tenor saxophone solo in Lionel Hampton's "Flying Home," affixing a single note to the music behind every other beat.

They are warnings, or challenges, or alarms. Those repeated notes are the performer, or the subject of the song: they represent a person, a will. Again, those notes played several times, or many times, don't amount to repetition for repetition's sake; they are temporary interludes. They don't lull the listener or fully take him somewhere else. When a musician temporarily stays close to a single note, it might make the musician and the listener more alive. (Stubbornness is best expressed by a musician playing something that has not been notated or fully predetermined. This is why it's different from the multiple E-major chords played solemnly in the two beautiful "Louange" sections of Messiaen's *Quartet for the End of Time*. They express something else. Fate, maybe. Not the question of the immediate present.)

The stubborn note, for the listener, is its own phenomenon. When you listen to a single note sounded repeatedly and temporarily holding court, you are listening to either a form of resistance or play—or resistance *as* play—but not the language of dutifully developing and then circling back to sum up.

It could be a human's short imitation of a bell. John Lee Hooker recorded a beautiful song, "Church Bell Tone"; it begins with four detuned notes on the guitar's string. It's about a death. His woman is dead. Why is she dead? "She been mighty low." Where has she been, where is she going? "Way down in shady land." The song begins with uncertainty: he thinks he heard a church bell tone. The bell represents the woman. He is coming into consciousness about the woman. The bell is reminding him. He thinks, and then he knows. Hooker did a lot with stubbornness. He wasn't necessarily imitating eternity. He worked within small frameworks. He used notes rhythmically, and he sang songs that often had only one chord. "I *know* I heard a church-bell tone this morning," he concludes. "I said bye-bye baby, bye-bye baby. I know we'll never meet again."

Why a bell? It is strong and resonant, a sound with body; it suggests a soul or a being. (In "Herod 2014," by Scott Walker and Sunn O))), a faint bell can be heard nearly throughout the track, there but not there, sometimes almost totally obscured by the song's other events; it represents the embattled character Walker is singing about. In the film version of *The English Patient* the sound designer Walter Murch introduced a single bell tone—unrelated to the script or plot—just before the war-veteran title character begins the first of many flashbacks. That was only one bell strike, but the bell was the patient.)

Aren't bell tones usually predetermined? Yes, but unless you're already looking at its clock, a church bell always rings by surprise. At the first sound, you're startled: *Be on your guard.* Something has officially begun or ended. Perhaps something has been punctured or hurt. (Other single notes heard alone: a bottle being opened; the screech of tires; a gunshot; a body hitting the floor.) Then you hear the second one, just like it, and you notice it's the same. By the third you know the pattern, and you're aware what the sound is, what it signifies. You are halfway to understanding why it's happening now. Everything else you were taking in before—voices, machines, the buzz of electricity—recedes into silence. Edmund Burke, from *A Philosophical Enquiry into the Origin of Our Ideas of the Sublime and Beautiful,* 1757:

> It may be observed, that a single sound of some strength, though but of short duration, if repeated after intervals, has a grand effect. Few things are more awful than the striking of a great clock, when the silence of the night prevents the attention from being too much dissipated. The same may be said of a single stroke on a drum, repeated with pauses; and of the successive firing of cannon at a distance . . .

(He meant "awful" in the archaic sense: bringing awe.)

The stubborn note is bossy; it takes you over. It puts you on notice. It is a marker, a reminder: wake up, get free of your momentum, you have somewhere to be right now. The difference between this and true repetition is that repetition puts a spell on you. The stubborn note takes a spell off you.

———

Many gods have been worshiped to its sound, and the repeated single note is itself a kind of supreme being. The closer you get to church, the more the single note is accepted without question or surprise.

In other ways, the single note can create a risk. Because the listener may struggle with it: Am I going to allow this to happen? Is my intelligence being insulted? I came for a meal; this is only the starch, or the stock, or the salt. Is this kind of playing a lack of generosity or intelligence on the part of Johnny Ramone or Arsenio Rodríguez—because he didn't have time or energy or material to give us any more than this note or phrase, or so much of it? Or is it the opposite: that he thinks highly enough of us—he loves this, this is his distillation, and he is truth-telling, trusting we can take it?

The repeated note is often the tonic note, the home address of a melody. Solos bearing down on the tonic have the honest charm of a person who never shook off the speech and manners of where he was born. Or they're a kind of intellectual breakthrough: they put forth the possibly brave understanding that we don't necessarily have to keep changing for the benefit of a consensual ideal. It's okay to stay at home; it's okay to keep doing the thing that you like, that you understand, that you do best.

And of course when a musician revisits a note, he is being generous, anticipating a desire: in this way he gives you, the listener, time to get to know it. ('Tis the gift to be simple.) You orient yourself around it. You get to hear how it sounds in different areas of the beat, played with slightly different emphasis, against different chords. Arsenio Rodríguez was blind, and as an improviser he could be imperious and controlling. In "Cero Guapos en Yateras," he wasn't just playing hypothetically, or following a script, but prodding the other musicians, making them change course with his stubbornness. In the middle of the solo, when he grows most commanding, the band doesn't take the cue; they're just vamping through, not realizing that his repeated chords are a command to go somewhere new. But then they seem to realize, and thereafter, they follow him, even as he changes the structure of the song, moving the chords down by half steps, as if the song were sliding off the table. The listener feels his strength, and possibly even his frustration. And this makes the song an event.

The composer La Monte Young, who has performed a lot of music based on single chords held for a long time, has said: "When there are long sustained tones, it is possible to better isolate and listen to the harmonics. The harmonics can assume a greater relevance to the fundamental musical material, allowing [the musician] greater opportunity to work with them and to produce other tones which are related to them." The words in brackets are mine. I assume he meant the musician. But he also could have meant the listener.

When we listen to music, we are often making music ourselves, in a parenthetical sense. Especially if we're talking about popular music, in which the listener's identification with the musician or singer is so directly on offer, so much the point. (This opens a chicken-or-egg question: Was it mass media that created the universal listener-performer identification, or pop music? At a certain point, the music hastened the media.) When a listener lets the music in, the listener embodies the music. He lives waking life with an earworm, or he moves at a club according to the information of a groove, or as a member of an audience he will help establish the tempos and dynamics of a band's performance. In any case, feeling the rhythm is not too far from playing the rhythm, and one's response to a repeated tone is to replicate the tone for yourself, hold it in your head, think along with it or sing along with it, and experience the musician darting above it and below it, putting it against other notes and chords.

This is especially a good way to hear Rodríguez or the singer Ismael Rivera, who, in his early-career records with Cortijo y Su Combo, didn't often stay locked on a single note but often implied one with many:

those notes, plucked or sung, are so gorgeous, so swinging, so strong and sure and individual, real as rocks. There's nothing automatic or contrived about them. (The notion of "inevitability" is one of the most direct ways to take the measure of any music, improvised or written. Do the notes sound like they *had* to be played?)

What happens when the listener puts these experiences together, making one long chain of single notes? In 2011, David Readshaw Barclay, an oceanographer from San Diego with a history of acting on little ideas that were meaningful to him and distributing the results online—for example, printing T-shirts with drawings of pairs of film actors he had confused—compiled a list of songs with one-note guitar solos, and issued it as a 15-minute cassette called *One Note*. The track-list included Neil Young, of course, four times; Aztec Camera's "Oblivious" and the Ramones' "Sedated"; the Coasters' "I'm a Hog for You Baby" and Dr. Feelgood's version of same; Brian Eno's "The True Wheel"; the Who's "I Can See for Miles," Katrina and the Waves' "Walking on Sunshine"; Creedence Clearwater Revival's "Tombstone Shadow," Slint's "Good Morning, Captain"; Edgar Blanchard's "Lawdy Mama." He cut one solo into another for the most part without fade-outs or overlapping: it became one long single-note solo, an unbroken line changing color and width and touch.

Some will find this goes without saying, but *One Note* is hard to listen to. It's a series of rigorous self-inspections, for the musician and the listener. It keeps patting you down before abruptly shoving you to the next checkpoint. Over and over, it gets very close to you and then suddenly doesn't know you anymore.

THELONIOUS MONK, "Thelonious," from *Genius of Modern Music, Vol. 1*, 1947

JOÃO GILBERTO, "Samba de Uma Nota Só," from *O Amor, o Sorriso, e a Flor*, 1960

NEIL YOUNG AND CRAZY HORSE, "Cinnamon Girl," from *Everybody Knows This Is Nowhere*, 1969

MODERN JAZZ QUARTET, "Pyramid," from *Pyramid*, 1960

THE RAMONES, "I Wanna Be Sedated," 1978

AZTEC CAMERA, "Oblivious," 1983

ARSENIO RODRÍGUEZ, "Cero Guapos en Yateras," 1946

DRAKE, "Furthest Thing," 2013

FLOYD DIXON, "Let's Go Smitty," featuring Johnny "Guitar" Watson, 1959

LIONEL HAMPTON, "Flying Home," featuring Illinois Jacquet, 1942

JOHN LEE HOOKER, "Church Bell Tone," from *The Country Blues of John Lee Hooker*, 1959

THE COASTERS, "I'm a Hog for You Baby," 1959

BRIAN ENO, "The True Wheel," from *Taking Tiger Mountain (By Strategy)*, 1974

THE WHO, "I Can See for Miles," 1967

KATRINA AND THE WAVES, "Walking on Sunshine," 1983

CREEDENCE CLEARWATER REVIVAL, "Tombstone Shadow," from *Green River*, 1969

SLINT, "Good Morning, Captain," from *Spiderland*, 1991

EDGAR BLANCHARD, "Lawdy Mama," 1958

7. Elevation

Virtuosity

I have in my head an assertion that a friend once told me was written by Whitney Balliett, the jazz critic and exemplary listener-describer. The assertion was that there were only two absolute virtuoso figures in jazz: Sarah Vaughan and Art Tatum. When did Balliett write it? I can't say. Neither can I be sure that he did write it. Once you get inside a writer's voice, you can imagine things he didn't actually write. Once I troubled Whitney, in his old age, about a phrase of his I swore I had read—something about Lester Young playing "wheaty" notes. He said it sounded possible, and went to look it up. He searched for a couple days and came up empty-handed. I might have dreamed it.

If he wrote the bit about virtuosity, the statement would have been heavily qualified. Look through his work and you see that he called many musicians virtuosos: Coleman Hawkins, Benny Goodman, Dorothy Donegan, Louis Bellson, Charlie Shavers, Al Gallodoro. (I had to look up Gallodoro: clarinetist with Paul Whiteman, said to have played the introduction to "Rhapsody in Blue" more than ten thousand times.) Virtuosity is not a measurable achievement. It is a distinction conferred by others. There are either millions of virtuosos or very, very few. Who knows? But it persists, the only word we have in the language to denote a very special class of musicians.

No matter. I feel that I've read it elsewhere: the idea that Tatum and Vaughan were the two defining examples that established the type in jazz. Let's not proceed from the assumption that Balliett said it, or even if he did, that he was right. Let's treat it as a straw argument: a way into the question of what a virtuoso is, how special the distinction might be, and how we meet them with our hearing.

Jazz is an art of surprise and charm and learning and tradition and invention and survival. It is often entered into by musicians who might feel that their gift is too large to be contained by pop or the church or classical music. Tatum and Vaughan may have been prime examples of such musicians, but there have been other kinds, too, untouchable yet closer to the ground: Louis Armstrong and Charlie Parker, John Coltrane and the young Chet Baker, Max Roach and Oscar Pettiford, Oscar Peterson and Chick Corea and Peter Kowald. On the Tatum-Vaughan level elsewhere: Jimi Hendrix and Beniamino Gigli, Kendrick Lamar and Pablo Casals, Camarón de la Isla and Sidiki Diabaté, Beyoncé and Chet Atkins, Lil Wayne and Marcus Gilmore. (No prominent composers in that list. Composition often involves other people, and often involves revision. I set aside here consideration of the composer as a virtuoso creator as distinct from being also, sometimes, a virtuoso performer. I am concerned here with only the kind of virtuosity that exists in one musician, unfolding in real time.)

Are the truest virtuosos complete? They seem to want to be, don't they? They want to surround you and spread their shadow of certainty over the entire history of their form. Do they have everything? Not always. Uncertainty can create extraordinary knowledge. Great skill can block uncertainty. Sarah Vaughan and Art Tatum didn't have everything. They didn't have the chain of sidestepping strategies that comes with modesty. They weren't great at yielding and undercutting themselves. In performance they were perhaps more formally subtle than honestly subtle.

Maybe there's a reason so many true virtuosi are religious. Perhaps they can't contain their own pride and gratitude, or they can't house the gigantic battery needed to power it. They need an external storage space for it, and they call it God. Necessarily, some other force powers the show. And then they may be released. They don't need to spend time justifying their efforts and staying on top; they can just do their job, which is to satisfy the desires within the audience that they have already created.

What we hear when we listen to Sarah Vaughan and Art Tatum is, first, confidence. They are operating within traditional boundaries; you know, when you hear Tatum's galvanic runs between melodic lines, that these are established flourishes, a legible language of show. In the hands of lesser players, these runs might serve as an insurance plan in case the playing is elsewhere not excellent; but lesser players wouldn't want to endanger their functional playing, the kind that serves the direct ends of melody, harmony, and rhythm, by making such an elaborate ornamental gesture.

I do, sometimes, find something corrupt about scalar runs or long arpeggios that aren't actually necessary to connect chords within the music, those that extend for a half measure or more and appear to have no function. The moment that swagger begins to feel mechanical— which is to say perfunctory or nonpersonal—I can feel I'm being condescended to. I think this is what Bob Dylan was talking about in a recent speech when he voiced his skepticism about a version of "The Star-Spangled Banner" he'd heard sung at a boxing match by a "very popular soul-singing sister." (It was likely Marsha Ambrosius at the Mayweather-Cotto fight in 2012.) "She sang every note that exists and some that don't exist," Dylan said. "Talk about mangling a melody. Take a one-syllable word and make it last for fifteen minutes. She was doing vocal gymnastics like she was a trapeze act." If I can imagine a perfect response to this comment, it would be Marsha Ambrosius recording a forty-minute version of "Masters of War," a cappella, full of intent, for home listening, and full of as much melisma as she likes.

But it is worth questioning whether there is an exclusive relationship between lack of flash and truth or honesty. Tatum worked those runs so deeply into his strategy of playing, as in "Sweet Emmelina, My Gal," recorded for Decca in a Los Angeles studio, and "Sweet Georgia Brown," live at Monroe's Uptown House in Harlem, that he made them personal. Really, you stop noticing them; they're the meat and potatoes of his playing, far less remarkable than the other things he's doing—changing harmonies, setting off fireworks that keep signaling a false end or a real new beginning.

The truly great flatterers are mostly working for themselves, expanding the territory of their own greatness, even as they seem to confer dignity. Likewise Sarah Vaughan: Why, especially after the 1950s, does she put so many different timbres and attitudes in her voice? Why the formal silliness, the cloying little-girl affect and the exaggerated low notes, below her comfortable register?

She's showing you just how much she contains, according to an index specific to jazz and American pop up till then, with all of its role-playing, border-crossing, and transgressions—women singing like men, whites singing like blacks, grown-ups singing like kids, Americans singing like the English. I am listening to her singing the ballad "Time After Time," from *Sassy Swings the Tivoli*. It's a set piece, very slow and quiet. She's setting up the theater audience—and you—for privileged listening; the tempo and the hush becomes the cushion for her very expensive voice to rest on. Perhaps she is trying to make, by comparison, Frank Sinatra's 1946 version of the song seem homely, and his 1957 version seem square. She is trying to be in an elevated place—higher than her contemporaries, higher than you.

The first line ("Time after time") starts very late, thrillingly so, in a mild baby voice; the second line ("I tell myself that I'm") comes in exaggerated false Cockney, ending in a perfectly controlled and extended vibrato. Then "so lucky to": "to" and "you" stretch out five seconds each. She gets in deeper. "So lucky to be the one you run to see in the evening": by now she has taken leave from the song, more or less, and will for the next few minutes. She's in her own chamber, and doesn't come back to it until the band double-times into easy swing, three minutes into a five-minute song. She is moving around, changing her strategies, all in the defense of her voice—the right for it to be considered on its own, almost to the exclusion of other music.

All this wild maneuvering is the price of the ticket we must pay to absorb the resonance Vaughan could put in a single note. Sometimes the overabundantly talented can seem to be reflexively pleading their case in a cold room, as if listeners are the jury, and we have arrived with doubt.

Well, sometimes we have. When we listen to virtuosi we are often waiting for fact and evidence. If Tatum can do one of those punishing runs, let's see him do it again to make sure it wasn't a trick of circumstance. A virtuoso, the listener feels, can always do it again. (There is a special subset of recordings in the world whose great qualities seem to be unrepeatable, particularly good because of some electromagnetic or psychoacoustic or otherwise physical strangeness, something about the musicians' bodies and the spaces they inhabited in that time and place: *Eric Dolphy at the Five Spot*, Al Green's *Belle Album*, the slow Sarabandes of Maria Tipo's Bach Partitas, Cannibal Ox's *Cold Vein*, *Sylvia Rexach Canta a Sylvia Rexach*. All of them are special, all are accomplished. None of them are virtuosic in the truest way.) And so Yma Sumac sings through her battery of larynx and respiratory devices; the Turkish singer Hamiyet Yüceses, in her great performance of "Bakmiyor Cesmi Siyah," executes the most fantastic curves and trills and slow revelations in her voice, measuring and extending her breath in ways that we may find unthinkable at first and then codified, repeatable, official, so that we're almost disciplined into admiration. Sensing the audience's cruelty, the virtuoso can develop an imperious streak of her own.

One doesn't only find virtuosi in show clothes and in guaranteed-private dressing rooms. They need numbers, and the way toward instant crowds today is on YouTube. Handheld-camera gospel videos are a fascinating subset of Internet artifact: Ocie Jackson, from Milwaukee, encountered in the halls of a church and asked by friends to sing a few lines of a song, knowing that she's showing her excellence, her modesty not an issue because she's singing for a higher purpose. Or the many videos of gifted teenagers singing spirituals in a car on the way to church, the camera bouncing at stoplights and traffic signals. They're not quite rehearsing; they are always performing, not just with their voices but with their eyes and faces and their breathing, always half-aware that a camera pointed at them means posterity. This is virtuosity in its purest form.

The same ends, to a lesser extent, are served by YouTube shred videos, which are so nearly alike as to become ritualized: a boy alone in his room, sitting on the edge of the bed, mimicking whatever guitar soloist he most loves that day. It's a thoughtlessly public sketchbook, or temporary marker of adeptness. But many musicians need reasons to practice, inspirations for competitive improvement, elevation to a performance that *can* be repeated. For some the threat of nasty commenters, and the desire to quiet them, may be enough.

Listening is a creative act, and at a certain point it, too, can be virtuosic. In short, that may mean listening to virtuosos and learning about what, exactly, they are doing. But at length it means developing a heightened sensitivity to current and past standards of excellence, and to the moments when virtuosity transcends established language, when it becomes weird. Because it often turns out that what makes

Sarah Vaughan truly great isn't the range of her voice, her diction and expressivity, or how accurately she can jump octaves. It is when she can puncture formalism and make you want to weep, when you can only guess at her motives for doing something or other, because the degree to which virtuosos are undefinable is the degree to which they are great.

This happens quite a lot when you listen to Sarah Vaughan. Sometimes it isn't even triggered by a virtuosic moment at all. In "You Hit the Spot," it is the casual way she pronounces the word "spot." The idea of someone satisfying her needs fully is a profound one, but the phrase is a common cliché, and she knows it, so she can't make it sound fancy. She plays at trying to. Virtuosity needs banality to act as its mirror, to license its extraordinariness.

In most kinds of music there is no tradition for virtuosity being a ground, basis, or starting place. And that accounts for most of the problems that there may be in listening to Sarah Vaughan and Art Tatum. They start from virtuosity. Their ability seems to outrun the musical material they're working with. (Neither was much of a composer.) And in the open valley beyond their great ability is only their own self-indulgence.

Virtuosity is the most misunderstood quality in music, and our response to it as listeners makes us take a position toward it. Such as:

Virtuosity is bestowed by God.

Virtuosity is in bad taste.

Virtuosity is generosity.

Virtuosity is inessential: more than speed, or range of power; it's superfluity.

Virtuosity is striving with economic implications. Virtuosos with a well-tended gift get enough work even when they don't get enough respect. There is a bottom line of ability and value in virtuosity that can't be contradicted. It's very clear what the terms are when you listen to

Tatum or Vaughan or Vladimir Horowitz: the audience must be delighted. The audience pays to be delighted because most of the rest of life is toil and disappointment. And so the virtuoso's job remains secure as long as the audience has a precise and reduced expectation of what art is supposed to do for them. A would-be virtuosic marching band in Texas to which I once became close always began its halftime show with a version of the theme song from the television show *Entertainment Tonight*. "We do that," the drum major told me, "because we're saying to the audience: you're going to be entertained." People need to be told, sometimes.

This is old news. All artistic impulses—even the oldest ones, of pure documentation (we were here once; this mark on the rock proves it) or reenactment (we once did things this way, and are still trying to understand it), are predicated on stopping the flow of time and giving you a new perspective on living. Immobile art forms—drawing, painting, sculpture—freeze time and let you walk around the artifact. Music opens up a door, moves you through an alternative time-grid parallel to the life of obligations and immediate needs. And so music can be a relief, or a corrective balance. You can see what role virtuosos have in society: they are gift givers. To experience them is a reward, something to look forward to. When you are listening, you are a virtuoso yourself; momentarily, art has nothing to do with toil. It's just speed and flash and triumph. And generosity, perhaps, but also something more glamorous than any idea of generosity can contain.

But what if music, and art in general, isn't separate from life but actually part of it? What if bills, territorial disputes, doctor visits, and deadlines aren't the stock of life but merely equal parts of it, along with Horowitz and Tatum and Vaughan? What if music isn't a gift and a relief and something special in life, but actually necessary to consciousness? What if music teaches you qualities of motion, ethics, ambition, in the most basic sense? What if it encompasses both an inner will to understand and an outer will to flatter, convince, and dominate?

Well: then virtuosos are star lecturers, and it makes sense that the decline of the lecture in American education has been coterminous with the decline of the virtuoso. They won't teach you how to be, or how to find your way within the subject. They won't teach you what music is for. They might do something else, though: they might stimulate you so that you, later on, can find out what kind of musician you are, or what kind of listener you are. They are the son-et-lumière projected onto the pyramids of Giza, a facsimile òf inspirational awe set against slow millennia of learning and understanding.

ART TATUM, "Sweet Emmelina, My Gal," 1940

ART TATUM, "Sweet Georgia Brown," live at Monroe's Uptown House, from *God Is in the House*, 1941

SARAH VAUGHAN, "Time After Time," from *Sassy Swings the Tivoli*, 1963

HAMIYET YÜCESES, "Bakmiyor Cesmi Siyah," from *Women of Istanbul*, c. 1940

8. Blue Rules

—————Sadness

When we listen to Nick Drake's record *Pink Moon*, if we know anything about the person who made it, we are probably hearing through a layer of sympathy. If we're listening out of choice, we probably know this man died young. We may even know that *Pink Moon* completely qualifies as "late work"—an unsentimental production full of nothing-left-to-lose moves: uncomfortable repetitions in short songs, snippings-off before a smooth finish, a disembodied quality to the singing. Just guitar and voice, close miking, no band, no strings, no reverb, some buzz on the guitar here and there that might in more closely watched circumstances have necessitated a retake. In other words, what we often think of as "truth."

We might know that Drake died from an overdose of mood-regulating medication not too long after the record was made, depressed and to some degree unrecognized. We might think, logically, that his last songs are like last words—a suicide note or a will. Or that they came from a small life-force within him that couldn't be destroyed, some part of his sensibility that could remain playful.

And when we listen we might think about the most vulnerable aspects of our own sensibilities, too—the irremediably blue parts, the hopeful parts, the shy or naïve parts. We're respecting, we're salaaming. If we have made our way to *Pink Moon*, many of us are not only guarding ourselves against specific calamities, disappointments, or embarrassments, rites of passage that we will inevitably face, whoever we are—missed deadlines, bounced checks, the trials of school and money and love and work. We are guarding ourselves against death. We are getting the most out of this piece of music because it represents an achievement reached while life was at stake.

We're pretty used to this idea, even though it is by no means universal: whatever tendencies or tensions a serious artist may have had earlier in life, his late creations bring them out in stronger terms.

We do a lot of extra work in our listening around the notion of sadness—a phantom quality in listening that most of us nonetheless recognize and agree on—and through our extra work, we become especially vested in the music. The extra work takes the form of myths that we build around the reasons and circumstances of a recording, and through that myth-building we temporarily disbelieve in artifice. Artifice is the practice and process of being something one is not, and it is used to small or large degree by every artist in the world. It's as transcendent as truth.

But sadness portrayed in music, whether the zombified reserve of some English bohemian folksingers during the 1960s—Nick Drake, Jacqui McShee, Vashti Bunyan—or a sustained low note on a cello, is Lethe water: you recognize the symbol, drink it as you listen, and you forget all possible practical circumstances around the sadness you think you're hearing. These can be the musician's desire to connect with the tradition and audience of an earlier musician, and thereby to have his work accepted more quickly and earn some money; a producer's desire to add emotional variety to an artist's work; a singer's decision to use a different part of his voice or capture it differently through microphones; or a fully contrived aesthetic absolutism equating misery, integrity, and obscurity—the Romantic era's interest-bearing gift to the future.

On the listener's end, the circumstances adding up to a "sad" listening experience can be practical and not sad at all: the need for a focused and isolated stretch of time that is all his; the need for a bracing effect in order to focus while doing something boring, like being in transit; or the need to reenact the emotions around something awful, which paradoxically makes you feel alive: a death, a breakup, a rejection, a failure.

The myth of Nick Drake, assembled posthumously by those who didn't know him and are willing to sustain romantic theories about him, is that his music hinges on, and is more or less about, fatal disappointment and the desire to disappear.

But I have never felt very sure about that.

When you listen to "Road," from *Pink Moon*, you're listening to craft and technique and a series of choices. His long fingernails are precisely picking a steel-stringed guitar with unusual tuning: several strings are tuned to the same note, so that among the different fingers you get a spray of notes that sound huddled close together. You are listening to his papery voice, just above a whisper—though that is a trick, too: good performers know how to project and sound confiding. And you're listening to rhythm, his thumb lining out the downbeats with a sharper picking sound as well as the mellowness of the voice, working against the slicing sound made with the hands.

And then there is the fact that what he may have been intimating and what he may have felt are different things. Sadness can be generative. But depression is uncreative, shapeless, mute. Nick Drake may have experienced depression earlier that day, or in that general time of 1971, but everyone does in a general time, to some degree. It doesn't seem wrong to say that "Which Will," from *Pink Moon*, on its vocal phrasing alone, is not the sound of active, real-time depression. There is too much swing in it.

What is sadness in sound per se? Nothing. It doesn't exist. There is no note or kind of note that in and of itself is sad and only sad. (Heard differently, Nick Drake's voice can also be relaxed, or tired, or content.) But the construct of sadness, and the attendant contract that it helps build between musician and listener, has to do with how we might recognize it person-to-person: through silence and dissonant long tones, or through agitation and mania; through closed systems of harmony or phrasing, or through unnervingly open and dark ones. We hear it through voices and through instruments. And as listeners agree to play by the official rules of sadness, so do most musicians, and so do most singers, imitating the sound of instruments.

But of course not every thin voice or descending melodic figure connotes what a work of music is about; it's case by case, with the meaning suggested by tonal relationships within those figures, and all the context around the figures. (The Adagio-Allegro movement of Mozart's String Quartet no. 19 includes various descending figures; the first ones, slow with small dissonances in an indeterminate key, sound sad; the later ones, up, brisk, major, sound happy.)

The writer Albert Murray, in his 1973 book *The Hero and the Blues*, expressed the idea that the blues wasn't an act of sadness, but an act of defiance and survival; that the great skill of black American culture was the ability to improvise a way out of the suicidal impulse. It seemed counterintuitive at the time: weren't there plenty of examples in black American music of voices or instruments that were actually mimicking the sound of crying or disappointment? (Billie Holiday's "I'm a Fool to Want You," Etta Jones's "I'm Through with Love," Robert Johnson's "Stones in My Passway," Howlin' Wolf's "Smokestack Lightning.") But Murray was probably right. Bent notes and in-between notes, the key ingredients of that music, can't be notated, because they're not clinical examples of music; they're clinical examples of living and minute-to-minute choice. They cut unusual paths. They are not singing from the page; they're full of individual will. Listen to that music thinking not about sadness but about achievement and ambition and invention and care, all the things that tend to run counter to sadness, and it makes much more sense. It's not instinctive moaning, the sound of someone running out of options, ready to curl up and die. It is learned excellence.

There is one sense in which I think Murray was wrong. There is a culture around any music, and how you understand that culture influences how you hear. Listening is augmented hearing, hearing through certain layers. Sometimes music follows a consensual code from maker to taker: hearing through an intellectual filter, in accordance with somebody who's playing through the same intellectual filter. The filter doesn't have to be sincere or true. Sometimes it can be a managed lie. But the mood survives, passed on and on.

Flamenco, similar to the blues, is often a song of defiance and resistance, sometimes of boasting or the maintaining of human standards; it is the music of poor people memorializing, or taking a stand on everyday things that cause anger and defy logic. But it is almost unbearably tempting to call it all sadness. Partly this comes from performance style: flamenco singers—Manuel Agujetas, for a good example—look like they are going to burst, and sing that way, too; they rise to the sort of shouting that can ruin a voice. And the fact that the music rarely changes its basic harmonic vocabulary suggests an extramusical idea that things will not get better, that the cantaor understands the notion of eternity and is squaring off against it.

There is no more variegated and better developed code of sadness and fatalism, and probably no better managed lie, than in heavy metal. The music itself developed in response to a modern understanding of sadness: the "chronic ennui cycle," a theory that runs from Evagrius to the nineteenth-century French Romantic literary critics—Baudelaire, Sainte-Beuve—to the time when Black Sabbath was kicking in to the culture. The extreme subgenres of metal over the last forty years can be seen as different stages of the ennui cycle: anxious boredom, objectless anxiety (black metal); frantic activity (death metal); numbness (drone or doom metal).

Metal is the fanatical generation of myth. It holds the unthinkable in hysterical awe. It runs on fear but looks like greed. It's all inverse gospel, and the code for listening to it is as complex as gospel's. It doesn't give you false assurances. It tells you that wars will continue. It tells you that flooding and plagues will continue. After Slayer's *God Hates Us All*, there's really no room for songs about human oppressors. (After Slayer's "Flesh Storm," there is no room for songs about the media: it describes press coverage of war and atrocities as addiction and vampirism. "The cameras are whores / for the daily bloodshed / like a junkie / hungry for a fix of anything.") It wants to pull the listener down into the earth, which is of course what will happen to the listener eventually. You will find its makers warning, repeatedly, that there is not a complete intellectual framework for everything. You cannot understand the world. The closer you get to the extreme kinds of metal, the deeper you look and listen, the more the lettering appears drippy and cryptographical, the more the music sounds smeared and scratched, or massed and indistinct, or too fast to register.

It is concerned with limitations, but not "I can't run five miles this morning"; not "I don't see myself as a mother, I'd prefer to be a favorite auntie"; not "I had four last night, got to stop at two." Not even "I can't bring myself to say thank you." Limitations as in: What kind of order should we bother to create in our lives while knowing that human existence has been bitter since the paleolithics? When does permanent mourning become a temptation toward the opposite: loving death, encouraging its approach? And, in extreme form—wishing for putrefaction: How can I get some?

To steady themselves in the world, metal bands ransack various bodies of thought that seem epic or esoteric: the book of Revelation

(Iron Maiden), Sumerian myth (Nile), H. P. Lovecraft (Metallica). It changes at the exact rate that its players grow too old to perform. On its official surface it has almost no concern for what is new.

Metal makes very little happen in the world outside itself. Imagine how powerful a kind of music could be if there were no separation between stage and floor—if the listeners were as heroic as the performers. That is the case in metal. And yet it's not an agitating force. In its radical forms it becomes general and indistinct, by its own will. It engenders half-formed philosophies, an optional resentment of the rich, an entitled slouch or a frown worn like a conqueror's pose, a highly calibrated melancholy. Its listeners trust in one sure sense memory: they like having their heads done in by the resonance of a drop-D chord or a blast beat. (In drop-D tuning the lowest guitar string is tuned down a whole step. A blast beat is claustrophobia in rhythm: strings of sixteenth notes on the snare, kick drum, and cymbal at the same time.) Metal engages a physical placement of the listener: it pushes him down, cloisters him tightly, shakes him up.

Reacting to music physically is a social response, the only real reminder we have of a time when music was by definition made by musicians in front of us. Metal listeners always will. Banging your head is simple and serious. It's the only thing to do. Your feet anchored to the spot, your forehead leading the way in understanding the downbeat and the sentiment. You are a shareholder. The body's response to metal isn't just about sound, but about existence: *Yes, it is this way.*

Most people see only its aboveground sprouts. They see long hair, beards, black clothing, military boots. Slack and frowny faces. Pale bodies, undernourished or overnourished. Young people traveling in groups, unclear about whether they're frightened or they want to frighten you. Or, down the history of metal as mass-culture show business, they see even more ridiculous things: leather and chains and furry chests, cocaine hair, operatic wailing. But it is metal's prehistory that keeps it moving. Its roots extend to fire and plague myths;

thousands of years of wondering what goes on, in this life or any other, below the ground; the psychological condition of acedia (later characterized as the sin of sloth); and the notion of the sublime.

Punk is busking and journalism and dogma and accountability and unity and the humanities. Metal is virtuosity and philosophy and disposition and rumor and misanthropy and science. It is both higher- and lower-class than punk. It values virtuosity, as a practical matter, as pure get-me-out-of-the-projects striving. At the same time it chases after highly abstract and almost decadent notions about darkness and blasphemy. It's not always smart, and it is seldom very kind, but it tries to feel inevitable. It wants to rule you.

Metal is weighed down with ideas, with all the burden of being heretical. Every band, song by song, album by album, has its agendas, its concepts, its intent. We are not worried about that. We are worried about the larger issue—the message in the music alone. And the music is pulling at you, hysterically claiming you. It goes long, overplaying its hand. It is vulgar, overstated, repetitive. All this is built in to the beginnings: Black Sabbath's "War Pigs" stays in one chord for a long time, and in a single couplet rhymes "masses" with "masses." It is setting up absolute conditions: it is not to be taken lightly. Either you will listen to this with fundamental enthusiasm, making your life around it, or you will have nothing to do with it. That's fine. That's good.

And that's the best way to listen to Celtic Frost, or Enslaved, or Yob: alone, but feeling that you're part of a group based on common interests that go beyond music. The reason that there are so many kinds of metal, wide enough apart that you can like some and not like others, is that metal is a disposition. It's deep hysteria—the rightness of being fundamentally wrong. And like all great contradictions in music— like complicated simplicity, or agitated joy, or jaded youth, or artful sloppiness—it pulls listeners in, makes them want to make sure they understand. It makes us listen harder.

NICK DRAKE, *Pink Moon*, 1972

MOZART, String Quartet no. 19, Quatuor Ebène, from *Mozart: Dissonances*, 2011

BILLIE HOLIDAY, "I'm a Fool to Want You," from *Lady in Satin*, 1958

ETTA JONES, "I'm Through with Love," from *So Warm*, 1961

ROBERT JOHNSON, "Stones in My Passway," 1937

HOWLIN' WOLF, "Smokestack Lightning," 1956

SLAYER, *God Hates Us All*, 2001

SLAYER, "Flesh Storm," 2006

BLACK SABBATH, "War Pigs," 1970

9. Getting Clear

━━━⟿⟿⟿━━━ Audio Space

When you hear Roy Haynes's drum sound on his album *Out of the Afternoon*, the beats themselves can't be abstracted from how they are echoed in the room. As you listen, you think of the shape of the space in which the record was made, and you think of what that space looks like and feels like, and you make associations with that space.

It sounds like a space with a vaulted ceiling, which it was: thirty-nine feet high, with wooden slats making a cathedral shape over the drum area. Even for a record engineered by Rudy Van Gelder, who owned the studio and worked with some very powerful drummers there, this is an unusual sound. Beyond the fact of the physical dimensions, the drums are mixed high in the recording, and especially on the snare and bass drum you hear a fair amount of reverb.

Not an excessive amount. There isn't a nebulizing after-report rising off every stroke; when Haynes plays his dancing patterns on the cymbals, you hear them accurately. The sound doesn't travel on and on in a way that contravenes reality—perhaps it suggests a slight exaggeration of reality, something that you might hear in an actual enclosed space, if it were thin and tall, shaped like the head of an axe. You can find yourself unusually aware of these drum sounds, almost as if you're inside them. And being inside them in this case means being above them, floating on the ceiling, because they suggest a vertical space and a rarefied position.

Things are very clear up here, in the land of "Moon Ray," the album's first track. Your own thoughts become quickened as you listen; you feel your appetite returning, you have the welcome sensation of knowing what you like. It's a privileged and clarifying position. "In the attic, fears are easily 'rationalized,'" wrote Gaston Bachelard. "In the attic, the day's experiences can always efface the fears of night." "Moon Ray" is a good illustration of that thought.

A record like this makes you understand music as a representation of physical space. Music is thought of as primarily existing in time; that's what defines it philosophically. But it also exists in spatial relation to the microphone or the ear, and most of the advances in production and audio technology have had to do with making elements of music sound like they're in your face or down the hall or next door, around you or evenly before you, flat or tiered.

The Who's *Live at Leeds* communicates a sense of music reaching its physical perimeter and scorching it. You hear it in all the breaks of "Young Man Blues," the cut-off chord Pete Townshend plays before each new verse sung a cappella by Roger Daltrey: an echoed, abrupt seventh chord—*brap*—and all those cymbals, constant cymbals. The mix is extraordinary: loud and near, except for all that echo around anyone's singing. The guitar sound has body and presence but the vocals have a distance which keeps them imposing.

Because of how they boom and resonate, and perhaps because producers tend to suppress their power rather than encourage it, the drums can imply physical space with inspiring directness, particularly the bass drum, and particularly in the right place and circumstances. No other element of sound that eliminates time and space that way brings you into a sense of physical familiarity with the room, even if the music was recorded before you were born. It is in Billy Griffin, the drummer on the Impressions' "We're a Winner," and his great funk playing, the sexiness of his foot making patterns around the crack of the snare. The sound of John Bonham's bass drum has it in Led Zeppelin's *Houses of the Holy* and "IV" and *In Through the Out Door*, though nothing I've heard conveys that sound so well as a recording of him alone, laying down a track in a reverberant studio in Stockholm in 1978: the bass drum comes first and most significantly, the basic unit of the beat. Everything else organizes itself around it. (Others have done similarly: Greg Errico of Sly and the Family Stone, John Stanier in Helmet and Tomahawk, Kyle Spence in Harvey Milk.)

Paul Motian was a special case. He used space and silence so that everything he did on the instrument, including on the bass drum, became equally important—parts of an unfolding event. He didn't let the bass drum dominate; he dominated it by detuning it, so that it splatted. In the last ten years of his life, because he almost always played in the same room—the Village Vanguard—he calibrated the splat to the dimensions of that space.

Motian often recorded for ECM, which has put much of its record-label identity into the notion of audio space as an end in itself. What it does may be little more than a classical-music recording aesthetic applied to jazz: there is always some kind of reverb, and always a feeling of separation between the instruments. And sometimes the musicians chosen by the label's founder and producer, Manfred Eicher, are naturally drawn anyway to slow tempos and the sustain pedal, both of which manufacture the feeling of space. Paul Bley, who recorded one of the first solo improvised albums for ECM, has said that the invitation from Eicher came at a time when he was "trying to be the slowest pianist in the world"; that tendency might have been an outgrowth of having worked with electronic instruments, which led him toward the possibility of artificially long sustain.

———

When you listen to music, do you want to feel that you're in a particular kind of physical structure or landscape? A cathedral, a cube, a club, a desert, a marketplace? Or do you want to understand space in relation to the music being played? Betty Cantor-Jackson, the Grateful Dead's live recording engineer, has said this about her preferred sound mix: "I want you to be inside the music; I don't want stereos playing at you, I want you to be in there, I want it around you . . . When my mix is right, and the space is properly formal, or should I say expanded, I consider that place as getting 'clear'; when I'm really clear, I can walk around between the instruments." Her mixes are remarkable for the separation and space among the music's elements, and what seems like an architectural arrangement of them. In "Dark Star," from the August 27, 1972, Grateful Dead show in Veneta, Oregon, the keyboards sound like a retaining wall for the rest, which is spread out before you in the right channel, present and articulated and sturdy, in a kind of low semicircle.

Both Cantor-Jackson and Eicher, interestingly, have talked about the beneficial pressure of recording one-take music—concerts, for Cantor-Jackson, and studio recordings, for Eicher. The Jamaican dub producer King Tubby did this, too, in his own way, making new paraversions of vocal hits different enough to feel valuable on their own, varied enough to keep hips and bodies engaged, and dynamic enough to make his records ring out into the night at outdoor dances—through a truck-bed sound system, all deep bass, echo, and cutting crash cymbals. He didn't achieve his dynamics via composed sections or instruments, but through live mixes of prerecorded material. His art was predicated on quick ideas, on shifting, staying in motion, in order to inject space into the music. He made his mixes directly to tape: what he did is what you get. That's what gives them their urgency.

Here the ethic of improvisation spreads to the engineer, to the producer, and finally to the listener. Something Eicher often says—or not so often, but often enough, when he consents to an interview—is "Think of your ears as eyes." That's part of what we do when we consider audio space in music. We have no vocabulary for aural distance; mostly we only talk about volume. Here, we're not talking about volume of sound, but volume of space.

I am listening to "Party in the U.S.A.," by Miley Cyrus, produced by Dr. Luke. It's a song about being young and naïve and deposited into a place with a presumed higher level of sophistication about culture, particularly musical culture: the narrator is a Nashville girl being taken to a party in Los Angeles. The party is above her level. She's closed up with fear; she lacks cultural self-confidence. And then, hearing what she likes, acknowledging it through repetition—not twice but, crucially, three times ("when the DJ dropped my favorite tune / and the Britney song was on / and the Britney song was on / and the Britney song was on . . ."), she finds a tunnel in the music. ("Nodding my head like yeah / Moving my hips like yeah.") It's a song about biding time with low expectations—apprehension, doubt, second-guessing—before entering a physical space of great possibility, and then, once inside the physical space, gaining psychological entry to the music that thrills you. Finally, it is a song about listening: one of the greatest ever made.

It begins with chunked rhythm guitar and moves along with medium-tempo funk drums, tambourine, and the most amazing synthetic swell in the chorus—distended, overmodulated, bass-thickened *bloop* glissandi that seem to bulge out of the wall, preceded by hissing and shooshing, pushing against your ear. Dr. Luke's signature is compression, which means a narrowing of the dynamic range of an audio signal (such that the soft sounds and the loud sounds are both loud). So rather than only flicking between soft and loud—which is what we once got with gamelan ensembles, Beethoven, and Nirvana, and what we have long accepted from composers as a useful method of playing with the listener's emotions—the song flicks between cluttered and uncluttered, or compressed and less compressed. Its softness is fake loudness. Its loudness is only slightly less fake loudness. It all feels close to you, but when it's really close, it's almost disturbingly so.

Producers and mastering engineers of the pre-'90s mentality often warn against compression for two principal reasons: because it erases the thrill of real dynamics, which is probably the first and most crucial element that anyone notices about music of any kind; and because it leads to what is now called "fatigue," meaning that the ear and brain can't distinguish nuances on a record, and finally can't accept any more information at a sustained level. But I think this ignores how the power of a song like "Party in the U.S.A." draws on its own suggestion of audio space—fake or not, fatiguing or not. It finds new criteria for dynamics, possibly forcing you to think beyond merely loud and soft.

An earlier, precompression example of space in music might be Pink Floyd's *Dark Side of the Moon*, from 1973, a record designed to portray movement around an audio picture. On *Dark Side*, all sounds seemed to become visible as well as audible. It had some things in common with "Party in the U.S.A.": the emphasis on sudden swells, enveloping sounds, a sliding guitar glissando instead of a synthetic keyboard one. The record is about the passage of time and memory; so it is likewise about encountering new things and leaving old things behind. And the effects on the record—in the intros and outros, outside the meat of the songs—affirm that notion. There are back-masked cymbals rising up in the mix like sudden geysers; audio recordings of planes flying overhead and other doppler, phase, or panning effects, strobing alternately into the left and right sides (as the producer Teo Macero had bounced John McLaughlin's guitar-playing among channels a few years earlier, on Miles Davis's "Go Ahead John"); hectic mixes, like the one in "Time," with its distant drum kit, water-wave background-vocal oohs, and hyperpresent organ; the sudden doubling and tripling of vocal tracks; the cross-panning journey of the delay-repeat keyboard phrases in "Any Colour You Like." The sounds are often moving toward you quickly and audibly receding from you.

A self-titled record from 2013 by the American-Japanese drone group Ensemble Pearl, which includes the guitarist and composer Stephen O'Malley of the band Sunn O))), seems an update of Pink Floyd's ideas of space without the songs. The notes—on malleted cymbals, on loud electric bass, on echoed and phased and tremoloed electric guitars—move away from the position of their sources, the places where they're struck or strummed, and travel outward in sustained ripples; the cycles continue until something alters your perception of space again. In "Painting on a Corpse," it's a sudden entry of twin jets of feedback at a level louder than the rhythm cycles, and then another entry of something else again—a stick or a bow dragged across a cymbal—at an even louder level. In "Wray," it's a close-miked viola string rubbed and bounced carefully and slowly over a bed of guitar tones treated to sound like vibraphone bars, or resonating glass bowls. Having listened to the mysterious, heavily echoed glassy guitar tones for more than a minute—it's hard to know exactly what made them or what was done to them—you're conditioned to think of them as loud; the tiny blips of gut string may not be louder, but they are clearer, more distinguishable, more present. You experience them as physically closer to you.

Likewise in "Brando," from Sunn O)))'s collaboration record with Scott Walker, *Soused*, a first guitar line sounds broad, cool, and majestic, at one with the wide-angle Bierstadt grandeur of the mix: Walker's operatic voice belting "Ah, the wide Missouri / Dwellers on the bluff" with an organ-in-a-cathedral sound. Then a second guitar line responds, nearly 20 decibels louder, distorted and staccato, uncool, drowning everything else out, implicitly humorous. (It's like an oaf stepping into a film shoot and blocking the camera lens.) These aren't just two sounds: they are two characters in a drama, a kind of disembodied opera, with dispositions of sound standing in for characters.

Both Pink Floyd and O'Malley—Teo Macero, too—got some of their ideas about audio space from the electronic and musique-concrète composers, including Pierre Schaeffer and Karlheinz Stockhausen.

(Teo Macero studied with Henry Brant, some of whose works using acoustic sounds in real time and real space—such as *Ice Field*, for one hundred musicians and church organ—were so enormous in aural-spatial scope that they couldn't be adequately recorded.)

Stockhausen's thirteen-minute *Gesang der Jünglinge*, from 1956, seems on some level an effort to compensate for its root elements: if your building blocks are only a boy soprano singing alone and sine-wave tones, and you want to make a music that's not defined by its material, you'd better figure out some great things to do with them. Stockhausen not only serialized the singer's tones—which is to say, he built a composition of ordered notes that used each of the twelve tones equally, making a music not specific to any key—but figured out a system to serialize the spatial elements of the composition, through constant edits. And thus what you hear in "Gesang" is an almost manic liberation from the I-am-sitting-in-one-place listening experience. You are hearing the boy soprano on the left, on the right, in an abrupt or slowly moving arc, at a great distance, up close. (It is surely part of our self-protective brain functioning that we tend to think of specific distances when we hear it: The boy is five feet away. He is six inches away. He is overlapping, in two places at once. We do this because we need to know how much time we have to raise our fists or run.) It is a recording that enlarges your sense of space, or of the possibilities that space can promise for music.

Perhaps he was thinking of earlier complex vocal music that dizzies the listener naturally, and suggests spatiality without special recording devices—such as Thomas Tallis's sixteenth-century motet "Spem in Alium," for forty voices divided into eight choirs, bouncing the different sections around. In a sound installation realized in 2001 called "The Forty Part Motet," Janet Cardiff captured each voice separately in a recording of Tallis's piece, and directed each through a single speaker. The speakers were arranged in an oval that the listener could pass through, creating spatial effects by walking and listening to the forty voices. Stockhausen figured out how to do it with one.

The safest place to be is up high. Let's get back to the attic. In 1966, TTG Studios, in Los Angeles, used eight tracks and tube circuitry for recording. (Soon, Tom Hidley, one of the engineers at TTG, would build one of the first 16-track, 2-inch tape machines. But he hadn't yet.) During that year, in March and May, Hidley recorded the Mothers of Invention's *Freak Out!* and the best parts of *The Velvet Underground and Nico* (the songs "I'm Waiting for the Man," "Venus in Furs," and "Heroin"). Those recordings sound like living beings today. The room was a rectangle; the ceiling was twenty-six feet high. Because the musicians didn't have to be acoustically isolated, as they soon would be with double the number of audio tracks, there were not that many microphones. The point is that in both cases you can hear broad, strange, surprising, jabbering music, with broad, strange, surprising, jabbering dynamics, interacting with the sound of the room itself. The air around the music becomes an almost tangible quantity, like the artist Rachel Whiteread's solid casts of empty space; the air suggests the dimension of the room, especially its height. Sometimes it does sound as if you're above the band: in the angry dance of the Mothers' "I'm Not Satisfied," the sinister drip of the Velvets' "Venus in Furs." As negative and paranoid as these songs can be—both these records invented versions of paranoia in pop that became persistent if not permanent—they sound high and summery, still. They efface the fears of night.

ROY HAYNES QUARTET, "Moon Ray," from *Out of the Afternoon*, 1962

THE WHO, "Young Man Blues," from *Live at Leeds*, 1970

THE IMPRESSIONS, "We're a Winner," 1967

GRATEFUL DEAD, "Dark Star," from *Sunshine Daydream*, 1972

MILEY CYRUS, "Party in the U.S.A.," 2009

PINK FLOYD, "Time," "Any Colour You Like," from *Dark Side of the Moon*, 1973

MILES DAVIS, "Go Ahead John," from *Big Fun*, 1974

ENSEMBLE PEARL, "Painting on a Corpse," "Wray," from *Ensemble Pearl*, 2013

SCOTT WALKER AND SUNN O))), "Brando," from *Soused*, 2014

KARLHEINZ STOCKHAUSEN, *Gesang der Jünglinge*, 1955–56

JANET CARDIFF, "The Forty Part Motet," 2001

MOTHERS OF INVENTION, *Freak Out!*, 1966

The Velvet Underground and Nico, 1967

10. Purple, Green, Turquoise

~~~~~~~~ Endless Inventory

There are various ways a listener can become a cognitive shareholder in the music he hears.

The simplest is by liking it a lot, or loving it. A small change in identity takes place. You become One Who Likes Song X, and if you take an interest in who the musician is under the performance, the voice within the voice, you might become One Who Likes Musician X. You may have tapped into something real there: not just a copyrighted melody or a product, but a human sensibility.

Another way of becoming a shareholder in a piece of music is by singing it. Another is by playing it with any instrument, acoustic, electric, digital. Another is by dancing to it in any way: with your feet, with your head, with your whole body. And another is by trying to own all of it, on recordings. Then you are a different kind of shareholder—a proprietary kind.

We can pretty much wave bye-bye to the completist-music-collector impulse: it had a limited run in the human brain, probably 1930 to 2010. (It still exists in a fitful way, but it doesn't have a consensual frame: there is no style for it.) It is not only a way of buying, owning, and arranging music-related objects and experiences in one's life, but also a distinct way of listening.

I think it's an upside-down understanding of what music is for. But

I also think it deserves respect for coming out of authentic human emotions: anxiety, sentimentality, infatuation, identification. It's different in spirit from the other kinds of listening discussed in this book: a vertical sensibility, following a single line through time, instead of horizontal, finding common points of reference across style and history. It might not increase anyone's listening flexibility in the short run. But it does quicken your attention for the long audition, and adds another dimension to listening. You are listening to hear life lived. You are listening to hear aging.

We listen for clues to how musicians think about their work in the large sense. Even the casual listeners among us can be pretty good at reading the signs of how much control they cede to other people. Mariah Carey's not a bad example of how this works. Her earliest music—particularly "Vision of Love" (1988)—had a private hungering force all around it. She was making a case for herself as a singer and songwriter. (She wrote some of her earliest hits with Ben Margulies, whom she'd known since her high school years.) And she was a virtuoso, doing extraordinary things with her voice, using the freakish "whistle" register, making one or many melodic runs out of nearly every line. It wasn't easy to imagine having her gift: she sent many young singers back to the practice room, including the young Beyoncé Knowles. The prime fact of a Mariah Carey record was Carey herself. The material, good as it could be, receded in her presence.

But then her work became backstopped by Tommy Mottola, the head of Sony Music and eventually her husband. By the mid-'90s her music became the leading example of pop/hip-hop constructions, with multiple producers and songwriters, four or five different names attached to each track, and that's what it was before all else: a notion evened out by a group. Finally she reached the decadent stage of pop. Her records were about her image; she appeared at the studio to put her voice in a preexisting mold. She may have been directing many things:

choice of collaborators, sequence of tracks, musical details. But it seemed that the music wasn't so much her own discourse anymore.

Through the 1990s, Marc Anthony made three promising-to-brilliant salsa records with the producers Sergio George and Angel "Cucco" Peña, in the twilight of musician-driven, popular, Latino-American dance music. When he later signed to Sony, Don Ienner—the Sony operative who signed him—was quoted in *The New York Times* as saying that his work for Sony would be collected. "The intent here," he said, "is to have a boxed set of Marc Anthony. We're not looking for hits—we're looking for history."

But Anthony had already been making history, and he became someone who thereafter made hits. Most of his new records no longer had much mystery in them. They had less middle, less tradition to engage with or argue against. Real pop destroys middles and traditions. (That is not a value judgment; that is pop's job.) The Marc Anthony Sony records, for the most part, have been Latinesque romantic pop records, less complex, each a freestanding product fairly independent from the one behind it or after it.

All of the above is not a complaint about Mariah Carey or Marc Anthony per se. They are still fine singers, and this is one way the world works. It's just an explanation of why comparatively few people might want to collect their albums—not merely to buy them, but to have them all in one place, to linger on them, to run back and forth through them, to establish continuities, to see what we may have missed.

Is it ridiculous to consider that anyone would ever want to do this with Mariah Carey? No. Thinking it ridiculous implies something else: it implies that music understood to be for dancing and comfort, music constructed to play on terrestrial Top 40 radio stations, isn't worthy of being collected, kept, and thought of as a corpus. That can't be right.

But why do we build collections? Perhaps we want to turn a musician's work into a living thing. We want to make it something to live around, rather than have it live around us. We want to corporealize it, give it a body and perhaps a soul. We want to have a relationship with it, as we would with a friend; or we want to codify it into a tradition or a belief. And at that point, when it is fully grasped and known, the work can be internalized for ever as an open question, a principle for living. Or it can be forgotten. A friend described to me the experience of acquiring a complete CD collection of Mozart, after having had a piece-by-piece relationship with his music for most of his life. It was 175 CDs, or something like that. "I realized," he said, "that now that I had it all, I never needed to listen to it again."

It's true that we can have clean, short, and ruthless relationships with our music. Sometimes we want legible and dumpable friends. But often we want our friends, traditions, and beliefs to be beyond understanding, to be a little bit opaque. If we can't completely read their signs, they will never cease to be interesting. We want to try to know everything there is to know about what can't be completely known.

When we sense that a musician understands music as a process without a fixed outcome, our ears notice two things: that we may not best understand his work in one song, one album, or even one period, and also that he probably believes his work may not be best understood in one song, one album, or even one period. At that point, we build our own mission as listeners. We put him in context, deciding that we only have limited room for him, or we totally submit.

It's the opposite of the hunger you may feel when the musician knows he's got a powerful thing and only gives you a little, leaving you hungry. It's the principle of the musician giving you a seemingly endless supply while also imparting to you the understanding that there is always more.

A self-contained hit single by Mariah Carey tells you that it's lucky if it gets to ride on your bus. But the Grateful Dead, Merzbow, Fela Kuti, and the Fall, for example, imply that you're lucky if you get to ride on their buses.

I never had the condition, but I consider myself lucky to have seen it. I remember my cousin's fascination with a single musician—Frank

Zappa—and marveled that he never seemed to listen to anything else. I watched a friend discover the Sex Pistols, about three years after they broke up, and reassemble their body of work: everything that was to be found, bootlegs, interviews, and side projects, before the Internet age. I knew a man in the early '90s who owned neat trays full of cassettes of Miles Davis concerts from the mid-'70s—a field of music only then becoming properly understood. He added more as they surfaced, like progressive tracework of a lost land.

Then I encountered the most widespread form of collector-listenership in America, the one that exists around the Grateful Dead. I saw form-fitting crates or attaché cases full of cassettes, each with the name of a concert hall and a date and "#1" or "#2" written on the spine. The J-cards wrapped around the tapes bore further categorizations and inscriptions, including the band's skull-and-lightning-bolt logo from the album *Steal Your Face* (the "Stealie"). Blair Jackson, the publisher of the Grateful Dead fanzine *The Golden Road*, has written about his own mapping method:

> As my collection grew, I joined the legions of folks who used custom J-cards. Mine had a discreet "Stealie" (without the lightning bolt) on the left-hand side of the spine, and I developed a color-coding system based on the band's different eras, using fine-tipped felt markers: '65–'70 tapes had a red Stealie and writing; '71–'75 were dark blue; '76–early '79 (when Keith and Donna left) were purple; the Brent era from April '79 until Jerry's meltdown in '86 were green; post-coma until Brent's death were turquoise; and the Bruce and Vince era had a red Stealie but blue writing. When I started my J-card system, I didn't know that within 10 years the purple on the spine of the late '70s shows would almost completely disappear, for some reason, and a few years later the green ones started heading towards invisibility.

Turquoise for the reanimation of Jerry until the death of Brent: that is love, and a kind of library science, but that is also listening. It is listening in the long view, with a basic understanding that the band's music only significantly changes when the body gives out; otherwise, that music represents one long discourse, all of it intrinsically valuable.

One listens to it all. That's not quite need, like breathing. It's an automatic endorsement through learned response, like morals and ethics. You don't strike a child, because you understand that the child has qualities that will redeem whatever he did that made you mad at him. He will be affected by your hitting him, possibly forever, and his eventual greatness of soul might eclipse yours. He is not a fact; he is a story, and his story is yours, too. To live is to follow that story. It is for reasons like that, possibly, that someone like Blair Jackson would not ignore the Bruce and Vince era.

But never mind Blair Jackson. This is how the average person listens to the Grateful Dead: we practice long stretches of suspended judgment until the group organizes its best potential. There are nearly 2,200 recordings of Grateful Dead concerts; most are at least two hours long. If you played them from beginning to end, continuously, through the night, it could take you six months to listen to it all. If you listened for two hours a day, every day, it could take you six years. That's not endlessness, but it is about as close as we have in a widely recognized corpus of recorded music.

The Grateful Dead's "Dark Star," live at the Rheinhalle in Düsseldorf on April 24, 1972, is nearly twenty-six minutes long. There is a "Dark Star" on just about every concert the band played during that spring tour. When listening to these versions of "Dark Star," from 1972, to speak of them in a collective state, you notice that the music tends to become nonlinear on micro and macro levels at around the ten-minute mark—there are many short moments of feedback, temporary dropouts of drums, a funny pulling apart of melodic patterns. Things get fluid and furry. The grid falls apart. On the music's upper levels, you hear a practiced uncertainty about how the song is going to proceed. The best versions of "Dark Star"—like the one played in Düsseldorf, which becomes harmonically and rhythmically abstract very quickly, and keeps tending toward successive waves of intensity—make the listener turn away from the music at a certain point and ask: What is happening? How did we get here? Generally, at the end of "Dark Star" there is a rejoining, resurgence, and solidifying—a lot of playing that implies victory and return.

There are 219 recorded live versions of the Grateful Dead playing "Dark Star" between 1968 and 1994 in known circulation. When you pay attention to each one, listening both for moment-to-moment detail and wide-angle structure—as much as such a thing is possible—you are constructing the most reliable readout of the band's collective energy and ambition at a given moment in its history. For the post facto listener—one who wasn't there, who can't will the band back into existence, who knows these performances only as catalogued, digitized, time-coded historical events—this has become one of the most important functions of "Dark Star."

The written, reproducible part of "Dark Star" is short. The idea of the song is that it's a question mark, an opportunity for the band to do whatever it wanted to do—a small concert in itself. It became a story with a familiar narrative: peace and home, war and travel, peace and home. Rest, activity, rest. Boy meets melody, loses melody, finds her again. Humans have an almost unlimited desire for stories with stock signposts, but built-in possibility for variation. Something's going to loosen somewhere after the beginning, and perhaps several more times thereafter, but when, and how? "Dark Star" follows the format we know best and most basically, our basic unit of conscious experience, health, and organization: the day.

Everybody's a connoisseur of days. We know that they are all individually different, that they can be compared only with imprecision. We struggle to compound and accumulate the knowledge we have made in days we have already lived; we remember peaks, or tell ourselves that we do, but often forget what is traumatic or unspeakable. (It is much the same with Grateful Dead recordings.) Connoisseurship means that we know when a day is more or less objectively great and yet we can't stand it, or when a day is poor yet we have a strange attraction to it. With the unit of a single lived day we can have a complete, 360-degree relationship: in anticipation, retrospect, and real-time actuality. Our more long-range thoughts, about the days we have not yet lived, take two mutually exclusive forms. First, that there will always be another one. Second, that they are not in endless supply. We can't do anything with this contradiction. And so we are almost primitively sentimental about days. We love them in a panic. We win every day, but we have always already lost. We want to collect days: we take pictures, we keep diaries, we text and tweet the world in order to mark our place in one of them. This is how some of us love the long song of the Grateful Dead, particularly "Dark Star," which seems to be a microcosm of the longer performances.

The Dead have not been in charge of all these recordings, only the performances. (Although increasingly the surviving band members *are* in charge of the recordings, as they slowly become "official" documents, prepared and annotated by historians and released by the Warner Music Group.) But they intuitively battled against the notion that the studio record is the most important end result of a band's work, and encouraged the notion that a band should be judged on the work that it does most—which, for most bands, is the work of performing. Phish played its first concert at the University of Vermont in 1983. In 1984, the Grateful Dead, Phish's direct aesthetic ancestor, having made it clear that it didn't mind audience members taping its concerts, made it a policy to give tapers their own section at concerts, behind the mixing board. And so there was, really, never a time when it was expected that Phish concerts would not be taped and that the band would not be understood, theoretically, in full. This is a distinct way to listen: with the knowledge that you can roll back from any spot in the band's daily work and take in the entire thing. I realize that I'm resorting to the language of looking—it's hard not to. The notion of a great visible corpus is at least as old as maps. The notion of a great audible corpus is very new.

In 2012 a Connecticut-based music journalist with a PhD in musicology named Mike Hamad, having stopped listening to Phish in 2001, had a midlife moment and decided to explore what it was he had liked about the band in the first place. With a similar patience and attentive energy that he had used to examine tonal relationships in the lieder of Franz Liszt, he started a project, for his own enjoyment, of listening to all of Phish's concert recordings in chronological order, and making engaged notes on all of them.

There were many stretches of music to be endured. But he was looking at the work of a band in the longest view possible, in a way that has not been possible in the past with regard to human consumption of works of art. When you read the catalog of ships in book two of Homer's *Iliad*, you let it wash over you: it is historical information and incantation, modular and perhaps expendable, but necessary for complete understanding of how Homer has been understood, if not what he was up to. Many who know the *Iliad* never read it. The *Iliad* is only one book, but there are 485 live recordings of Phish playing the song "Possum." It is only logical, starting from the assumption that every Phish concert is to be recorded and heard in full, that you can know the band correctly only if you have heard as many versions of "Possum" as you know of or can find.

And then Hamad raised his level of engagement: on his first playbacks of these live recordings, he started to make real-time graphs of some of the longer songs, and sometimes entire sets. His graphs were linear, to be read from left to right, each song never longer than one line of information on a sheet of paper. He could have rendered it in standard notation, but this wasn't that, of course: transcribing every note and rhythm would take too long, and couldn't be done in real time, which was part of the point of Hamad's exercise. (Because the performances were made in real time, they ought to be analyzed as such.) His primary interest was how the band moved harmonically within a given key or around a given tonal center, so he invented a form of notation that gave a certain prominence to chords as rendered by letter symbols, using arrows, descriptive notes, and flowchart symbols to connect them. (He also tried to represent changes in rhythm and instrumentation and tone and volume, and much else.) When each one was completed, he had a record of listening that was both as micro and as macro as possible, given the circumstances, the thickness of the pen he was using, and the dimensions of the piece of paper. In effect they are maps—a natural response to an almost unprecedented circumstance for listening. His maps are of single songs in a concert on one sheet of paper, and sometimes, in a series of vertical lines, of an entire concert on one sheet of paper. He hasn't yet mapped Phish's entire body of work as an atlas, though perhaps that is exactly what he will end up with.

This natural imperative toward documentation may be one of the many things that the Grateful Dead and Phish absorbed from John Coltrane—not explicitly, but interpretively. In his final two years, from 1965 to 1967, Coltrane reached a new level of trust both with his own music and with his record producer, Bob Thiele. He seemed to realize that music didn't need to have a clear beginning and an end; he created a new band and a new style that mostly disregarded thematic material and focused on sound. And so in the final stage he let loose, signing off on the release of a great number of documents—twelve records or record-length batches of material in two years. Toward the very end there may have been a practical reason for this: he was sick, and might have wanted to keep his band paid while he couldn't work. In any case, his decisions created a kind of lesson that would work its way into popular and experimental and cultish music, hip-hop and noise and jazz and black metal in the decades after. (One thinks about the long discographies of Anthony Braxton, Evan Parker, Prince, Wolf Eyes, Xasthur, Nurse with Wound, Lil Wayne.) Create, document, move on. Let the audience establish its relationship to your work. That takes care of itself.

Merzbow, born Masami Akita, makes torrents of music with no

arc. His many, many records and performances are collections of ar-
rhythmic electronic shrieks and shudderings, more or less lying outside of structure and narrative meaning. (I am speaking of recordings
such as *Oersted*, from 1996, and *Tamago*, from 2004. The exceptions
I know include drumming, either by himself, as with *Ecobag: 13 Japanese Birds in a Bag*—a thirteen-disc set—or by Balázs Pándi, as with
Ducks.) They're very loud. He doesn't particularly work with depth or
echo. Stillness and space are not important to him. He works only with
power and aggression, feedback and pulsation.

His work can seem impervious to the listener. You can't move to
it; it doesn't come with markers of anticipation or closure. It doesn't
breathe, particularly, or imitate human temper. It doesn't suggest what
you feel as it goes along. In fact, if anything, it throws you off, or tells
you to go away. Your relationship to it becomes completely one-sided.
(If you find that you like it, you might experience feelings of being
a martyr, a rescuer, or a flagellant.) Your feelings for it are those of
your own making. He doesn't seem to want you. He doesn't seem to
love you.

There is a candidly fetishistic element around his work: the names
of some of his earlier records were *Sadomasochismo*, *Ecobondage*, *Flesh
Metal Orgasm*, *Music for Bondage Performance*, *Pornoise*. (Later in life, in
the first decade of the twenty-first century, his titles have moved toward themes of veganism and animal rescue.) But what's most fetishistic about his work is the volume of it. Between 1980 and 2012, there are
more than two hundred albums, both studio and live, and beyond that
about a dozen box sets with between three and fifty discs in each. His
music seems to announce that it has no casual or traditional place
for the listener, but perhaps the answer is in those numbers—the notion
of the traceable corpus, the opportunity to map or collect.

Both listening to his records and soldiering through his performances ends, for me, with the same feeling of hurt and admiration
and, ultimately, self-reliance. There's no defined place to stand in relation to it. You fend for yourself. The Grateful Dead makes enveloping

narratives; Merzbow makes negative atmospheres. You don't disappear in the great beauty of them; you assert your humanity in relation to their blasted nothingness. And one way of asserting your humanity over his work is, of course, to own it. (The complete *Merzbox*, fifty CDs, can at this writing be bought on Ebay for $1,500.) One's interactions with his work can attain the level of a parable or a riddle: If you are bothered by it, you must own some of it. If you obtain it all, then perhaps it no longer has a function for you; in all ways but physically, it will cease to exist.

Fela Kuti's music has served some of the same purposes as the Grateful Dead's, although the impulse to collect it must of necessity be different, because he didn't spend thirty years touring, playing the same theaters and civic centers, establishing a circuit of places to play music and a steady conceptual frame for how to hear it. Beyond those who lived in Lagos in the 1970s and '80s, there is much less of a culture of having seen Fela. But his music, often in the service of human-rights protest against a military government, implies a story that will repeat.

I'm listening to Fela's "Kalakuta Show," a song about the police raid on his communal compound in Lagos, which he called the Kalakuta Republic, in 1974. After his saxophone solo and an establishment of a groove—pure James Brown guitar scratching with more bubbling drum patterns (and more drummers)—Fela suggests the presence of invaders. "One day, the whole thing change," he sings. "Dem do one thing dem never do before." The invaders cut the wire, break the fence, knock down the gate: people are running, heads are breaking, blood is flowing. In between verses, Fela, a human instrument, says, "Ah, shh . . . ch ch ch ch . . . ahh, oh . . . ahh, ey . . ."

It's a sustained show-don't-tell routine, an argument against definition and quick messaging. He indicates what's happening; by not interpreting it, by freezing us in the present tense of the attack, he is implying that this is what happens and what will happen, the natural state of things. The sustained groove, the fourteen-and-a-half-minute length, the rhythmic latticework and the I'm-not-going-anywhereness of it, all suggests that this is just part of a long discourse. Your listening changes accordingly, and the knowledge, should you have it, of the dozens of other comparable Fela records gives you a landlocked security. Likewise his "Zombie"—it's a system, but a system that's all middle, sinew and cartilage and tendons. It's rhythm latticework, with semiregular section breaks.

The point, for Fela and for you, is not to define oneself briefly within the music and get out. The point is to breathe and stay put. The implication of Fela's music—and the fact that he released nine records in the year of "Zombie," 1979—is that it will never be any different because it can't. The whole thing is long-view. It's surprised by nothing. If you are looking at one small part of it—if you favor a particular song—you are missing the point. The point is a larger array of music than the eye can see on the shelf, than the ear can take in within one cycle of memory. It doesn't reduce to a song or an album. It's a relationship.

The collected works of:

MARIAH CAREY

MARC ANTHONY

THE GRATEFUL DEAD

PHISH

JOHN COLTRANE

ANTHONY BRAXTON

EVAN PARKER

PRINCE

WOLF EYES

XASTHUR

NURSE WITH WOUND

LIL WAYNE

MERZBOW

FELA KUTI

11. I Forgot More Than You'll Ever Know

⎯⎯⎯⎯⎯~╫╫╫╫╫╫~⎯⎯ Wasteful Authority

As with any other form of communication, the voice contains more than one layer: text and subtext, what one says and what one means. But there is always a governing disposition of a voice, a speaker's true register. It gives the listener the real and complicated information, regardless of what the words convey. Constance Rourke, the great critic and explainer of American mythology, described the slow, high speech of the archetypal Yankee peddler this way: "as if an inner voice were speaking below the audible one." That's what I'm talking about.

There is a voice within the voice; the inner one is your aim, the outer one is your action. What can the inner voice achieve? Confidence and authority. In some cases, if you care too much about maintaining your authority, the outer voice translates your authority as weakness. When they are in balance, you can create a kind of playful distance from your own material, your own music. You've created a puzzle: an authority that you appear not to care about.

Since the 1990s, there has been a vogue among rappers, chiefly Tupac Shakur, for Niccolò Machiavelli's book *The Prince*. I wonder why it isn't another Renaissance book: Baldesar Castiglione's *The Book of the Courtier*, published in 1528. Machiavelli wrote for statesmen and diplomats and crime bosses: negotiators, doers. In a sense, Castiglione wrote for

Yankee peddlers—strivers who could be of uncertain or low-ranking origin, entertainers, those not necessarily born to power who needed to manage their connections with power in order to thrive. Rappers, and performing artists in general, are thinkers, watchers, absorbers. They represent diversionary commerce; they must win listeners first through art. It is only later that they can win more of them through business sense.

Castiglione used the term "sprezzatura," which means a cultivated indifference. It's the notion of "I could give you exactly what you want in the quantity that you want, and I might, but I will also show you how little effort that takes, and how quickly I will forget what I just did." It is a dark cousin of generosity, which is effortfully offering something of mutually agreed-upon value. It implies a seemingly impossible thought: that the artist doesn't even need an audience, or that he has been put in front of it by random circumstances. It is fantastically powerful for music.

When indifference animates the voice within the voice—when it is the core of any given performance, whether or not it is the artist's true disposition—then the artist can put nearly anything on top of it. It is not the only kind of authority, but it is a good kind.

Broadcasting this kind of musical authority doesn't only involve the hard, repetitive work of living inside rhythm and tone, finding your own balance, staying legible and in tune. It involves self-confidence so great that it borders on cynicism, and publicly limiting your romantic aesthetic ambitions. It involves playing to an audience's mistrust of art as an applied science or skill. It involves a show of not needing to be a "musician." It can involve one of the hardest and most heroic public stances, which is carving out a public space in which to be private: to be amused, to be slightly distant, to turn your song into commentary.

———

Tommy Duncan, the baritone singer for Bob Wills's Texas Playboys, had sprezzatura as much as any singer. He was nearly thirty when he became famous in 1940, when "New San Antonio Rose" became a genial virus across America, and even then he sang like someone who has seen death in his own clan. He was an observer. He had a flat face and small teeth and did not smile easily.

He sometimes laughed, in a private way, on the band's radio broadcasts. His 1946 version of Woody Guthrie's "Oklahoma Hills"—"Way down yonder in the Indian nation / Ridin' my pony on the reservation / In those Oklahoma hills where I was born"—is a performance with a subtext: it's about a man, Duncan, trying to get on with his work and remember his words as his boss, Wills, tries to knock him off course with interruptions and trickery.

What survives of Duncan's public persona on film, performing with the band, is almost slouchy. He wore a double-breasted suit and cowboy hat and sang in a gallant-homely voice, and moved as if he didn't need you to understand that he knew the score. He seemed to have gotten past wanting to impress anyone, or do more than show up for work and look out for himself. When he sang "Keep Knockin' (But You Can't Come In)," he wasn't joking. He would not grasp and curry favor with the listener. He was charming and polite and satisfied you, but kept you on the hook by not giving you exactly what you wanted. Wills, always, singing and playing fiddle, functioned as the group's hype artist, cutting through Duncan's performances with inside jokes, but Duncan would not play on them.

He was dynamic within medium territory: medium-loud to medium-soft. One of the most beautiful moments in American music comes a minute into Cindy Walker's "Dusty Skies," a song Walker is said to have written at the age of twelve. Living in East Texas, not far from the great plains region of the state, she heard stories of Midwestern dust-bowl farmers losing their land, forced to move by natural disaster: the mixture of drought, windstorms, and poorly nourished soil. "Dusty Skies" is a song of stoic terror, written from the point of view of a fleeing farmer. It is a marvel of form meeting content: the song itself doesn't seem to know where it's going. It ends on an unresolved couplet.

Wills's version of "Dusty Skies," with Tommy Duncan singing, recorded in 1941, makes miraculous turns into quiet. The band seems to bend toward him at these moments, and he delivers the lyrics as if the narrator must impart emergency thoughts that someone important nearby—maybe his children or his spouse—should not hear. Duncan sings:

> 'Cause all of the grass and water's gone
> We'll have to keep movin' on.
> Sand blowing, I just can't breathe in this air
> Thought it would soon be clear and fair.

Cindy Walker wrote the lyrics—at twelve!—idiomatically, but Duncan is unrattleable: he will not make them cute, he will not show you that he acknowledges the talkiness of the writing. He sings them as if he is making them up. This is a moment that tests him. He will not be arty. He is not locating a deep emotion within himself; he is reporting secondhand that one may be occurring.

A double act similar to Wills and Duncan's—trickster/straight man, manic/depressive—defined Dean Martin's stagecraft with Jerry Lewis. Dean Martin, obviously, had sprezzatura. The only thing he appeared to care about in his voice was his vibrato, which he downplayed anyway. Otherwise he was singing in the shower: his entire enterprise was ease edging into absence. Of his personal life, his second wife, Jeanne, remarked: "Dean can do nothing better than anyone in the world." His repertory—a little of which overlapped with Tommy Duncan's ("Please Don't Talk About Me When I'm Gone," "Corrine, Corrina")—was almost invariably either love songs or jokes.

Frank Sinatra had his own kind of authority, and far broader skill as a singer than Dean Martin, but he was sentimental about being an artist. He never questioned or denied his own ambition through his art. His music implies a total belief in his own earthly power, which is always a sentimental belief.

But Martin had more authority. None of his performances *particularly* stand out. His stubborn consistency is a thing to be awed by. He almost commands you to relax your standards, or to think differently about the purpose of art. Though he might not have admitted it, his music promoted hypnagogic thinking: like M. D. Ramanathan, the great Carnatic singer of Neelambari ragas, singing "Sri Jaanaki," Dean Martin singing a slow song ("If" or "You Belong to Me") might send you in the direction of pleasant, refreshing sleep.

He was natural at being adequate. The critic Brendan Gill was exaggerating, of course, when he described Martin as "the worst and most self-confident actor in the world." But he was also getting the point exactly. And in another sense the point was not even worth thinking about. Dean Martin made you not care what he did. He sang as if nothing was of any consequence. His delivery erases your memory as it goes along.

Still, a real integrity radiated from his singing. He appeared to be entirely game for artifice; he believed in lightness, in play. Not as a diversion, but as the thing itself, the heart of the artichoke. (As a work ethic, at least, if not as an artistic ideal.) As he performed—in the Martin-Lewis movies, on stage with Frank Sinatra at the Sands, on the *Dean Martin Variety Show*—he seemed committed to the idea of leisure. His, and yours. America had been a rough place until around the time he started singing. He is protecting your leisure. But beyond your right to comfort, you're on your own. The voice within his voice says: Suit yourself.

The force connecting Duncan and Martin, born in 1911 and 1917, was Bing Crosby, born in 1903. Duncan and Martin were each friends with Crosby, though not with each other. (In the 1950s, Tommy Duncan stabled his horse, named Bing, next to Crosby's; Martin followed Crosby's lead from the beginning of his life as a singer, to the days when they were fellow members of the Friars Club of Beverly Hills.) What they learned from Crosby was the stance of the dispassionate observer. In 1992, the clarinetist and bandleader Artie Shaw commented: "the thing you have to understand about Bing Crosby is that he was the first hip white person born in the United States." Shaw was talking about a particular kind of authority, the pose that can be learned only by imitating people with a cultural memory longer than documented history, the first people on a continent, those whose understanding of power goes beyond a single lifetime and isn't measured in numbers.

When you listen to Crosby, Duncan, and Martin, you have reached a place where you are welcome but not needed. You can tune out and come back. The art isn't measured out in three-minute segments; you're hearing a life's work taking place.

"Five Long Years" was written by the Chicago blues singer Eddie Boyd and recorded in 1952; it became one of the most common standards in postwar blues. The song intimates time passed, time squandered, the long wait of doing right and then the release of righteous frustration. It's wrong if it's sung too fast. Its best performances are slow: John Lee Hooker's lonely one, Junior Parker's lush and powerful one. The truest is by Muddy Waters.

Muddy Waters ran an interesting game. When he performed, the slower his tempos, the more commanding, imperious, and aloof his singing became. This was his disposition as a performer. But it's hard to keep that up in the long empty spaces left by a tempo of 45 beats per minute, and it doesn't pay to try. So in "Five Long Years," recorded live in Paris in 1976, he improvises through the song. He adds asides to the audience and the music itself; sometimes he doesn't bother to finish a word or phrase.

The song's narrator has been working in a steel mill; he comes home every Friday with his wages to be with his woman, until the woman doesn't want him anymore. Waters sings his response like this:

> [very quiet] I been mistreated.
> [loud] You, know! What I'm talking about.
> I, you know, I work—five long years for one pretty girl, peoples
> And she ha-aaaa . . . [trails off, high-pitched, into silence] . . .
>   put me out.

By whispering "I been mistreated," he undersells his allegation. You have to strain to hear it. Then he abandons the middle of the phrase "she had the nerve to put me out," as if he had a passing case of aphasia. This could be a way of representing the narrator's emotions: it's too humiliating for someone who's been abandoned even to say the phrase. But you can also read it as Muddy Waters's sense of control, and his aloof will to hold something back. The song would not exist but for a complaint, and so you expect to hear that complaint loud and clear. If he doesn't air it audibly, doesn't that erode his power? Not necessarily, not in music.

A similar expression of long-term authority comes from Mark E. Smith. As the front man of the Fall, he has been part of popular culture for thirty-five years, intersecting with punk and pop and techno, but he is still essentially a nonparticipant, a refuser to join. If he had kept a single band together, or even the core of one, he would have a trademark sound to protect. But he doesn't, really—the Fall denotes himself and whoever can work with him.

Smith has had a kind of leg up that Duncan and Martin and Crosby did not. In some sense he is working in the tradition of twentieth-century antisystem art movements—surrealism and vorticism, Beat poetry, early-'70s performance art, mail art. He chose to work against acceptance, whereas Duncan and Martin and Crosby presumably never saw any percentage in doing so. But they all share the ability to simultaneously inhabit their work and live outside it.

What he does in songs with lyrical hooks such as "Eat Yrself Fitter," "Kicker Conspiracy," "Slang King," and "Look, Know" makes the notion of "singing," or "lyrics," or even "poetry" kind of a joke. His art is not just commentary but a few steps beyond: imaginary newscasts, surreal ad copy. Commentary on commentary. He uses the patrimony of his culture (postwar English) and his region (Manchester): sharp ends of words, a rolling *rrr*, gallows humor, and the attitudes of orderly working-class pub-going life. He is resolutely local, dislikes trends, doesn't socialize with musicians, sends his mother to Blackpool for holidays. And he has laughed into his own tracks—sometimes voluntarily, sometimes not.

"Backdrop," a one-chord vamp from the Fall's 1983 live recording *Austurbaejarbíó*, is a superior song without a hook. Here is Smith at his best. It seems to be about the difficulty of becoming a proper adult surrounded by mediocrity in a welfare state, except that it is not political protest: it doesn't let the listener go so easily. It uses jargon and acronyms. Its aim is unclear, but its authority is not.

It is addressed to a "Leicester YOP instructor"—which probably refers to the Youth Opportunities Programme, a job-training measure introduced by Prime Minister James Callaghan in 1978, though it's up to you to figure that out. What's discernible of the lyrics is mostly derision. He mocks the instructor's "state-subsidized cannabis haze" and points toward the "backdrop," which he describes as shifting and changing. ("Movable!" he taunts. "Movable!") The backdrop, maybe, is time passing, and the instructor is not evolving at sufficient speed.

Smith pushes his flat voice until it squeaks like a child's; in the middle he forces himself to laugh, as a bitter *ha-ha* set piece, almost a part of the lyrics; and later, before the song's final crescendo and his intuitive attack on the keyboards—dissonant tone clusters, like what Miles Davis was doing with his band at around the same time—he giggles as he sings the most caustic and summarizing line of the song: "It's time you started thinking about the rerun which is your life."

There's nothing soft in the music. It has two drummers, one chord, an unskilled instrumental improvisation. It's long, and thickens with charisma and momentum in the last third. Its chastening spirit overflows. Its rhetoric does not invite you to come along for the ride, but its inner force seems sure that you will.

Laughing into tracks represents momentary authority—one passed from the musician to the listener and shared by both. Laughter is a denial of artiness. Lou Reed did it—in "Heroin" and "Temptation Inside Your Heart." Jimi Hendrix did it through most of "Crosstown Traffic." Joni Mitchell did it a couple of ways: her laughter at the end of "Big Yellow Taxi" sounds either nervous or perhaps arty-smug, the laughter of being on the right side of history. But her laughter during "In France They Kiss on Main Street"—on the line "raise Jesus from the dead"—is the real thing, her sense of remove from the task.

Fats Waller's entire act seemed predicated on the idea that piano-playing was not that important in and of itself. His playing has gravity and energy and beautiful flow; it's balanced and streamlined, and swings steadily. Waller seemed to understand tempo from the inside. Nearly all his performances sit right, moving at a rate that agrees with the songs' words and structure. (You can hear this not only on his famous recordings—"Ain't Misbehavin'" and "Honeysuckle Rose"— but songs such as "How Can You Face Me?" and "Up Jumped You with Love.")

But these performances are also very *light*. As the executive producer of his whole complicated enterprise, playing and singing and funny-voice-making and face-pulling, he makes the impact of his playing secondary. He can see beyond it. He seemed to be throwing away his talent. His attitude toward virtuosity is like the great Davis Sisters song: "I Forgot More Than You'll Ever Know About Him." Listening to Fats Waller is not a complicated experience. The extravagance and depth of it occurs to you only after you've finished.

Where is hip-hop in all this? This idea of suppressing or downplaying your own gifts as an indication of authority is not very popular in hip-hop. Hip-hop comes out of James Brown—not just his drumbeats, but the notion of earthly dominion as part of a guerrilla trick-bag, creating your own publicity because nobody else will. It comes out of Danny Ray, James Brown's tenured MC, who introduced him every night as the hardest-working man in show business. Jay Z may be analogous to Frank Sinatra, as the unseating of "New York, New York" by "Empire State of Mind" has proven. As it was for Sinatra, the story of his apotheosis is always with him. For the listener, Jay Z's story of Marcy Houses to corporate boardrooms runs as a constant parallel to his music, whether he's explicitly referencing it or not. It's all the Life and Times of S. Carter, and he validates deep ambition as artistic pose and heroic action.

But Lil Wayne at his best might have exemplified the idea more fully. His motivations are far less clear, or were, once—at least and especially during his greatest years, 2006 to 2008, when he was, outside of his own official albums, bleeding free downloadable mix tapes, supplying guest verses all over the place, working with a hundred different producers. He was confounding a bunch of basic and widespread notions: the capitalist purpose of hip-hop, the idea of a rapper delimiting and designing his own sound, and the idea of vitality, for here was a young man whose voice could sound like Redd Foxx.

He cut himself off, sounding strangulated, or as if the wind was knocked out of him. To punctuate his flow, instead of a full *yeahhh*, he said *ya—*; likewise he melted the ends off his own words.

("Mrs. Officer," 2008: "I know she's the law / She knows I'm the bo—" *Boss?* Probably. Or maybe not. This kind of detail became exaggerated and almost gothic in southern hip-hop: in Young Thug's "No Fucks," six years later, "I don't give no fucks" becomes *Aun geeah no fuh*.) He went deep into ridiculous conceits, just for the sake of doing so. His songs were cackled aberrations with dramatic turns into brilliance. He took his metaphors and similes to places where he was not welcome: he compared himself with menstrual blood, a tampon, a vagina. There was something wasteful or almost wild about it.

There might remain a collective will for Lil Wayne to make a great new album. But he may not, and since his sublime period in the mid-aughts has kept pouring out guest verses on other people's tracks—most of them containing some kind of wit in sound and word, but few completely extractable for their own value. His voice—only a bit less so since his court-appointed drug testing began in 2010—is a wheeze, a whine, nasal, phlegmy, needling. He sounds best when he's reciting but bored with the details—as if he's been doing this so long that he wonders why he needs to tell the tale, why he needs to bother with you. At these moments, like in "Sportscenter," his voice sinks by an interval of about a fifth in the wheeze, then rises again to start the new line. "Lookin' for a lady / High and sedated," he relates, as if this is the story of thousands of nights. He finds one.

> She gave me relations, so now we related
> the morning comes; the picture, faded.

Nina Simone made a spare record called *Nina Simone in Concert* in 1964: a trio at most, or just Simone by herself, live at Carnegie Hall. She'd been contracted to a new record label, Philips, and had made a decision to articulate the politics that had been lurking under the surface of her music. On the album, she sings several songs with her imperious, hard-to-track, wavering and wobbling voice—not liquid and not hard but somewhere in between, a gelatin or a colloid—that sound as if they belong in musical theater. They're songs to reward and compliment the sophistication of the audience. Either explicitly or implicitly, they deal with race trauma. The audience remains polite and effusive during the breaks, but there is a ringing silence through the songs themselves.

Simone is a cantankerous multiple-intent performer. The entire enterprise, of folk forms sung transformatively, messily, perhaps ironically, in a classical-music hall, describing oppression for the white upper-middle class, amounts to a mixed message. Listening to it turns on your doubt and surprise. Perhaps you can't imagine she wanted it this way. Perhaps you're surprised that she did. What's her percentage in it? Isn't she—as with Muddy Waters, as with Tommy Duncan—undercutting her own authority? Why does she seem so sure of herself? Why does she seem to step out of the song?

During "Mississippi Goddam," which disguises deep anger as musical comedy, she tells the audience, "This is a show tune, but the show hasn't been written for it yet." You can imagine Mark E. Smith or Lil Wayne saying that. But "Go Limp" is the record's weirdest and wickedest track, an exchange between a young, dim, female civil-rights protestor and her parents. Before setting off for an organized protest down south, the parents essentially warn her that she might be raped. She tells them they have nothing to worry about. At one point Simone sings the couplet:

> For meeting is pleasure and parting is pain
> And if I have a great concert, maybe I won't have to sing these
> folksongs again.

Simone is establishing her distance from the audience, from the song, from herself. She forgets two verses and remembers them later; one of them is the verse with the titular phrase in it. In a hard, hectoring voice ("Come on, now! Come on!") she keeps entreating the audience to join her in the singalong—"Toorala, toorala, tooraleye-ay." They don't really go for it. She didn't expect them to want to. The whole thing grows bitter in the extreme, tense and pedantic.

"Hm!" she says near the end, reacting to her own lyrics as if someone else had written them. "That's a funny song!"

BOB WILLS AND THE TEXAS PLAYBOYS, "Oklahoma Hills" (1946), "Keep Knockin' (But You Can't Come In)" (1946), "Dusty Skies" (1947), all from *The Complete Tiffany Transcriptions*

M. D. RAMANATHAN, "Sri Jaanaki," from *M. D. Ramanathan* (Nadham Music Media, date unknown)

DEAN MARTIN, "If" (1951), "You Belong to Me" (1952), from *Dino: The Essential Dean Martin*

MUDDY WATERS, "Five Long Years," from *Live in Paris '76* (Stardust)

THE FALL, "Backdrop," from *Austurbaejarbíó*, 1983

VELVET UNDERGROUND, "Heroin" (1967), "Temptation Inside Your Heart" (1968)

JIMI HENDRIX, "Crosstown Traffic," 1968

JONI MITCHELL, "Big Yellow Taxi" (1970), "In France They Kiss on Main Street" (1975)

FATS WALLER, "Ain't Misbehavin'," etc.

DAVIS SISTERS, "I Forgot More Than You'll Ever Know About Him," 1953

LIL WAYNE, "Mrs. Officer," 2008; "Sportscenter," from *Dedication 2*, 2006

YOUNG THUG, "No Fucks," 2014

NINA SIMONE, *Nina Simone in Concert*, 1964

12. Granite and Fog

〜〜〜〜〜⫴⫿⫶⫶⫴〜〜 Density

And now we get into one of the most mysterious properties of music, a crowdedness that we can't see, a proximity that we can't feel. By density I don't mean only demonstrable mass, something proven by numbers, a lot of notes produced by a lot of instruments. I also mean a quality of space: a heavy atmosphere, a force.

Outwardly dense music is often late-career stuff, overthought, unapologetic, a bit unbalanced. It's confrontational; it has a harder time getting on the radio. But I am listening to Outkast's "Rosa Parks," a hit from the group's middle period in 1998, and this is nonhectic density. The refrain "Ah-hah, hush that fuss, everybody move to the back of the bus" makes one rhythm; the acoustic rhythm guitar makes another; the frequent DJ scratching makes another; there's a digital drum groove with a pinging bass-drum tone, a weird sound on the two and four like a tennis ball being hit hard, two voices (Andre 3000's and a woman's singing "Ah-ha-yeah-yeah, baby, uh-huh") and, much lower in the mix, Andre 3000 chanting "lakalakalaka" and the soloing of an overdriven electric guitar. Dense.

The fact that fussed-over or premeditated elements are pushed down low, made to compete against one another for the listener's attention: that is what helps create density. The fact that there are four sources of rhythm: that, too. And so does the break in the middle, a psychological move in the form of a double-time, major-to-minor key shift from modern urban Atlanta electronic funk to a southern, country, small-group kind of thing, harmonica and handclaps: maybe five people, but you're up close against them.

When we talk about density we're talking about a concentration of things, of anything. Granite is describable as dense, but so is fog. Either quality is difficult to evoke skillfully in music. Action and counterpoint and speed and volume get you halfway there: within its first quarter especially, Beethoven's "Grosse Fugue" creates an almost impenetrably meshed atmosphere with its dozens of measures of forte or above, with its dissonance and mad plottings of interior lines. Big Black's "Passing Complexion," from 1986, with electronic drums, barking and trebly bass line, and rumbling guitar harmonics against a separate, chopping rhythm guitar line, sounds like four giant machines in a factory, heard up close. It sounds like something you'd need ear protectors to get close to. That's another kind of density, for sure.

Here are two other examples of the same principle—and again, not late-career, end-times provocation, just the work of imaginations that favored the density of one thing after another or on top of another, rather than a polished ongoing whole. Both are cover versions: they made an existing thing more complicated.

Chaka Khan's "I Feel for You," from 1984, written by Prince, produced by Arif Mardin. Twelve bars of rap including an introduction that sounds like a contextualized mistake, one bar of unresolved synth squeal including what sounds like another contextualized mistake, eight bars of Stevie Wonder's harmonica riff, two partial drum-machine high-hat patterns bouncing off each other in the left and right channels. Mostly synthetic sounds except for elements that Prince inscribed into the song: the slap bass in the passing chords during the chorus, bits of guitar obbligato, and the bright melodic riff. Stevie Wonder's harmonica solo, wobbling with reverb and delay. Bursts of sampled applause on the prominent one-beat, like a rattle from cymbal rivets. As the song ends, another out-of-context sample: a much younger Stevie Wonder singing "Say yeah!"

Sonora Ponceña's "Caridad," from 1969, a version of "Caridad Malda," from the previous year's *Patato & Totico*. In the best rumba sessions there are intense and sudden semi-intuitive shifts, when one kind of song becomes another as a new chorus starts up over the blurry agreement of hand drums working in polyrhythm. In "Caridad," Sonora Ponceña's arranger, the pianist Papo Lucca, wrote a formalized dance-band approximation of that shift, and added a few more. At first there is the sweet verse, hardened into commercial song, and then after a minute a full stop, and a change of key into a jam session: the main singer starts to improvise over Lucca's piano vamps. That could last for a while, but after thirty seconds there's another full stop. A new, more galvanizing piano vamp starts up, with a brass counterline: thirty seconds. Now the singer starts really improvising. Twenty-five seconds later: another stop. The song starts again at half tempo and gradually but swiftly accelerates: within ten seconds it's faster than it was, with a *mona*, an overlapping of horn lines, the singer now stretching out syllables and improvising more; after all that compressed activity—four full stops, a key change, a tempo change—the end feels free, flat-out, a glorious sprint. Because of all that you have heard, and how you have been conditioned to think of musical incidents within a time frame, you can take it in: you have been primed for maximum absorbency. You get all there is to get from the last thirty seconds of the song. You feel like you've lived in something! And when it's done, you can move on.

The foggy density can be much more mysterious than the solid kind, for obvious reasons. It can't be quantified as easily. It is there, but you can't point to it. It's made more of continuing tones—something that was there before and left a trace—than continually present struck or sounded ones. It's an atmosphere, not an attack. It is made of echo, which is an absent presence, like an imprint. It can suggest spirits in the room, many of them, generations of them. When music derives part of its power from a ritualized sense of family or tribe or ancient wisdom, and has been practiced in safe places in order to keep it alive with the knowledge that there are also unsafe places to practice it, that music is sure to possess some of this kind of density. Do you have to know the context of such a music to at least intuit the density of it? Do you have to know about persecution and history and old practices? I don't think so. I really don't think so.

I am thinking of "Mbombo Ya Tshimbalanga," recorded in 1969, by the Congolese bandleader Le Grand Kallé. Joseph Kabasele, Le Grand Kallé, came from the Luba people; Tshimbalanga is a Congolese name and place, and the song is named after an old Luba spiritual healer. There's a medium-sized dance band on the record: a lead and a secondary guitarist, two percussionists, a bass player, a trumpeter who comes in near the end, two singers.

Congolese and Senegalese popular music on record, around the end of the 1960s, can have incredible density: something about the recording equipment, maybe, but also about how individual lines of the music assumed position and then built up incrementally, occupying different parts of the sound spectrum, from the wide, deep bass notes to the chiming, high guitars. And also about how both cultures were reinscribing Cuban music. The wheel had turned completely. Cuban rumba derives from Africans in the slave quarters of Cuba; a hundred years later, Cuban music made deep sense to the metropolitan club scene of Dakar and Kinshasa. But the African musicians didn't just copy the Latin music of Cuba and New York. They excavated new chambers in it, found new ways for it to linger and resonate, brought an aerated feeling to it. Le Grand Kallé's band played many variants on Cuban music—which made sense, because of the Congolese origins in Cuban music—but this song is as much African as Cuban. It contains a huge area of both musical and spiritual culture, which ultimately helps give it a kind of authority, and a kind of mass.

The song is in a major key, gentle and sweet. First comes the vamp, shared between bass and guitar, big and mellow, resonant and echoing; then the drums and percussion tumble in weirdly, beating fast without a pattern, until the negotiation of a polyrhythm. Here comes the high guitar line, here come the words: the lone singer—Kallé Kabasele himself—against a chorus singing the subject's name. In the middle there's a short break of voices alone against the hard backbeat of the drums, a feature that might come from American soul music songs such as Otis Redding's "Shake" or Don Covay's "Sookie Sookie." A trumpet solo blooms, and then a guitarist plays a groove made of two chords separated by a half step, sliding downward into each chord. Suddenly the voices are all around you, in two sections alternating between notes, like the motion of a two-man saw. Kallé emerges from the mass to improvise rhythmically against the patterned voices. (The guitar vamp has basically never stopped.) In the thirty seconds before the fadeout, the cycles of rhythmic and melodic emphasis pull you in four or five directions at once.

There's some of both kinds here: the spacious density of the bass line and of the reverb and echo, and the different kinds of density that come from crowding and overlapping incident. The liner notes to the record tell us that this song was not a hit. Perhaps it was too dense. The last third, for sure, is contrapuntal jazz, layering for its own sake, experiment and play. Had the band used more instruments, it seems likely that the music would have grown even thicker. This is music in which a listener locates himself: first in a kind of open field, measuring just how far each of those resonant bass notes travels. And later through a crowded field, looking for openings through which to move forward with a hand or foot.

By contrast, Dexter Johnson, the Senegalese saxophonist and bandleader, was working on a density that was *primarily* spacious. In

Live à L'Étoile, from 1969, the band makes a giant throb of sound—a soft and roomy dance music. The bass notes sound vaporous; the movement in the music is cool and continuous, with no sudden or self-contained gestures. You can almost see it filling the space of the club, like a gas.

Many of the examples of density in European classical music—whether by "spiritual" composers or not—are a density of many voices, clashing tonality, counterpoint, speed. Olivier Messiaen's *Turangalîla Symphony*, for a good example. It's so big and churning. Even in the introduction—and certainly in the most organized high point of the work, the "Joie du Sang des Étoiles"—so much happens, by means of so many instruments: cymbal crashes, harmonized trumpet and tuba, lightning-hammer piano chords, glockenspiel, celesta, vibraphone, ondes Martenot, full string-orchestra chords. Its theme, we may find out later, is love, the kind that can't be contained or sublimated without dangerous or violent results. It's about an interior force that is not to be understood but which makes you larger, which connects you to things outside of it. And so the music describes such a force in kind.

The question is: Since music is not physical matter, what is more effective at slowing down the listener, surrounding him, entrapping him? Lots of layered bang-bang-bang, like Messiaen or Chaka Khan? Or one oceanic *vroooom*, like Dexter Johnson?

Like Le Grand Kallé, Miles Davis, on *Get Up with It*, did both. On this record are perfect examples of density of both kinds: "Rated X," on which he played no trumpet, and "He Loved Him Madly," on which he played only a little. Primarily you hear him on keyboards, on which he was not technically accomplished, which may be why these tracks sound like exercises in consciousness rather than in form. With the post facto help of his producer, Teo Macero, he made an extraordinary representation of getting outside of oneself, even if it wasn't done in real time.

"Rated X" is built of closely packed, overlapping tape loops; dissonant chords held on the organ; loud bass; a drum-set groove that repeats without stopping; hand drums over that; guitars comping with choppy wah-wah'd chords. (It is synthetic—it was constructed in the studio—but then again all recorded music is synthetic, processed through a nonhuman filter.) It crowds your field of listening: it disrupts the listener's perception of what's what and where and to what degree. Volume levels are suddenly boosted, certain layers suddenly cut out. It's unclear who's leading whom. The golem is surrounding you, but its head never stays fixed in one spot. This really is an experience that belongs to the listener: an explicit phenomenological experiment in the idea of density. It could not have been written, or played in real time, as such. One other thing is interesting about "Rated X": with instrumental music that involves various degrees of virtuosity, performances usually aren't so tampered with—stepped on, dissected, distorted. The artist usually remains more or less in control of how the recording sounds, because the artist is usually a musician who sees his primary craft, and that of his fellow musicians, as playing. Because of its method of construction, this isn't playing as much as turning phrases over to a fallible supercollider. These tracks are overloaded on the master tape; they bleed and rumble. Teo Macero was a musician, too, but "Rated X" suggests that his interests didn't necessarily align with those of the artist. He acted more like a listener.

"He Loved Him Madly" contains more of the Congolese/Senegalese kind of density, the misty kind. It is thirty minutes long and its first third is in free rhythm, with held keyboard notes and chords in the back, and half-articulated, fragmentary, echoed and multiplied guitar phrases. Seldom does the listener get so much of a sense of music as air. The air is heavy. Things are not moving much, but when they do, they move in triplicate. What is this? It is almost nothing, but it is vast. It's an atmosphere.

Some classical-music composers after Varèse and Xenakis have tried to work with the properties of sound as almost physical realities.

This can involve getting away from equal temperament—our common Western tuning system, twelve tones to the octave—and looking at composed music as sound spectrums rather than as notes on paper. It has involved nonstandard uses of instruments and also, sometimes, enormous ensembles, playing many, many microtones. Such works can be disorienting experiences for listeners: they seem to imitate nature, in their size and unpredictability, more than most other music in the world. Lots of instruments, lots of notes to the octave: you'd think this is a recipe for density without even hearing the music. And yet many works by these loosely affiliated composers (some of whom have been called Spectralists) don't give you what you'd expect: Horațiu Rădulescu's *Byzantine Prayer*, for forty flutes, is lovely and ghostly, like a chorus not of wind instruments but wind itself; Iancu Dumitrescu's *Pierres Sacrées*, for prepared piano and metallic plates, contains articulated representations of space.

And then, on the upper tier of thrills in the physical approximation of density, is Georg Friedrich Haas's *limited approximations*, from 2010. It uses an orchestra and six pianos tuned microtonally into twelfth tones—that is, 72 steps to the octave. With our standard system of equal temperament we experience sequential shifts of notes or chords as clear and measurable: we know we're getting somewhere. With so many tiny steps in between our standard semitones, a scale can feel to the listener less like a staircase than a ramp.

The piece spreads notes into orchestra-wide chords with subtle differences in pitch: it sounds teeming and vital and profoundly wrong, as if nature were a warped record. At an amazing moment not far into the second movement, the pianos start a downward locomotion, with the help of brass and percussion, making it sound as if the entire orchestra, and the listener with it, is going down a sinkhole. (The reverse happens halfway through the third and final movement: the listener feels gradually pulled upward.)

Several qualities help give this piece its physical thrills. There are sustained sounds—long, simmering string-section chords—and both wide and narrow intervals: the hammered chords sounding notes so close to each other that they sound like a gigantic out-of-tune piano, and the wide separations of pitch between strings, piano, and brass.

But most of us don't live such that we can appreciate a vastness full of particulars. We live and work and sleep and move in small slices of physical space: narrow streets, small bedrooms, transportation slots cut above and below cities. Our understanding of density is compressed to the scale of our lives.

And so we hear density more like Public Enemy's "Fight the Power," an elegant example from the just pre-lawsuit, early '90s peak of using looped fragments from other people's music: a James Brown rhythm section, two rappers weaving their lines, a depth-charge tone going off at regular intervals, and suddenly a pile of samples, such that you might not hear a given element until the fifth or tenth time you listen. It's a totality. Or we hear it more recently in Black Bananas' "Powder 8 Eeeeeeeight," bass lines worming underneath a saturated guitar, synthesizers twinkling and glossing over in messy battle. This recording does not suggest a congregation of spirits in the room. It suggests a pile of wanted and unwanted matter translated into sound, our treasures and detritus, everything in our lives with which we keep close quarters.

OUTKAST, "Rosa Parks," 1998

LUDWIG VAN BEETHOVEN, "Grosse Fugue," Takács Quartet, 2005

BIG BLACK, "Passing Complexion," from *Atomizer*, 1986

CHAKA KHAN, "I Feel for You," 1984

SONORA PONCEÑA, "Caridad," from *Fuego en El 23*, 1969

PATATO & TOTICO, "Caridad Malda," from *Patato & Totico*, 1968

LE GRAND KALLÉ, "Mbombo Ya Tshimbalanga," 1969, from *His Life, His Music: Joseph Kabasele and the Creation of Modern Congolese Music*

DEXTER JOHNSON, *Live à L'Étoile*, 1969

OLIVIER MESSIAEN, *Turangalîla Symphony*, Simon Rattle, City of Birmingham Symphony Orchestra, 2005

MILES DAVIS, "Rated X," "He Loved Him Madly," from *Get Up with It*, 1974

HORAȚIU RĂDULESCU, *Byzantine Prayer*, 1993

IANCU DUMITRESCU, *Pierres Sacrées*, 1991

GEORG FRIEDRICH HAAS, *limited approximations*, from *Donaueschinger Musiktage 2010*

PUBLIC ENEMY, "Fight the Power," 1989

BLACK BANANAS, "Powder 8 Eeeeeeeight," from *Electric Brick Wall*, 2014

13. As It First Looks

~~~~~~~~ Improvisation

The feeling of the truest kind of improvisation—an improvisation for its own sake, or one that doesn't follow obvious patterns—is the feeling of the most important song that has ever been made, built piece by piece in midair, after the jump and before the fall. It can be an absolute virtue: sometimes, taken in the right spirit of listening, it is not a question of how good an improvisation is but how improvised it is.

It means much more than it seems to. Improvisation is a metaphor for doing what you can while you can, for not waiting, for making use of what you've got at a given time, which can be an awful lot or a crucial little. It is, as has been said, composition slowed down. But it's also living sped up: the average decisions we make within the unit of a day about what to do and where to go, often compressed into a featurette much smaller than what we think of as a song, confined to the area of a single voice or instrument, or a group of instruments together. Oh, everyone improvises in some small way; there isn't a great deal of music that doesn't contain any element of choice or free will, at least in slightly rehearsed form, at least in tone, dynamics, or phrasing. But what we are discussing here is improvisation so forthright that it becomes its own subject.

A musician's impulse to improvise comes first from a sense of identity: in humans, or birds, it's what children do when they're already launched on their course of learning from a parent. They're learning how to talk in such a way that will broadcast their family, their tribe. At the same time, they are learning that the changing of a note can create a profound effect. Differences teach them continuities. Getting outside the patterns teaches them more about the patterns. Later they begin to understand that improvisation becomes a mode of survival, a method of showing power or flexibility.

But how much power or flexibility does a musician need to show an audience?

Improvisation can seem too individualized, too greedy, or too primal for mass consumption. There has to be a kind of superattentive, perhaps even slightly naïve culture of respect and achievement around a given kind of music for the truest improvisation within it to be appreciated. When a spirit of skepticism begins to collect around any style—What's the use of this music, anyway?—what is naturally spontaneous tends to retreat.

As far as the listener is concerned, on the basic level, music is only an extension of what humans already do without instruments. It's talking and walking understood through the ears, not through the eyes. As we listen we are profiling its makers. Is this person a friend? Can she be trusted? An improvisation will always fall short of autobiography. But it can get partway there: it is an unusually transparent work of the imagination. There is a persistent cliché about how all improvisations tell stories. Yes and no. For the musician, yes; for the listener, maybe not. We might not respond to improvisations strictly as a story, because we might not be receiving them strictly as such. But we may be receiving them as stories that we can't completely understand, in a language we don't speak.

There was a certain kind of performing personality in ascendance just as the recording industry was hitting its first peak, in the first two decades of the twentieth century. It was the broad-gesture stage performer, whether actor or musician, who wouldn't let you forget that you were watching a performance *worth documenting*—the performer as hero, at the time only recently able to be filmed, broadcast, beamed out to millions more than could fit in one room. This was the energy that Coleman Hawkins drew from: this, as well as the intensely dignified drive and articulation represented on early recordings of Bach by the cellist Pablo Casals, Hawkins's idol.

Hawkins's "Body and Soul," from 1939, is a sort of category-builder for listening to solos. It is a wordless two-chorus tenor saxophone improvisation, just over three minutes, with minimal backing; it involves a jazz ensemble but gives you one musician spotlit. Its characteristics are a tense tempo, a bit under medium; very little of the original melody, beyond the exposition in the beginning; an experience of depth and sophistication; and a self-conscious use of pitch, dynamics, and pacing.

"Body and Soul" is what could be called an "event" recording, the kind of thing that you might feel compelled to play for somebody else, watch her eyes, see where she blinks or smiles. But does it tell a story?

It can be heard as something like a door-to-door sales call that becomes a psychological exam. Hawkins plays the opening note three times, evenly, before he begins the melody proper: it could be a knock on the door, or a salesman saying, "Hello, ma'am." And he delivers the melody responsibly, in a sophisticated and casual mode, so as not to disturb or excite. He gains the listener's trust, and he starts enjoining phrases. Then he starts to use abstract logic and longer sweeps of music, growing more complicated but still not rising above a measured indoor voice.

The strongest moments of the solo come in the final eight bars of the second chorus, just after the song rounds two minutes and thirty seconds—so, about two thirds of the way through. They are the highest and loudest notes of the whole piece. In its placement of the climax, it aligns with the way many of us think narratives work, even if not any one narrative in particular. (Ernest Newman, in his book *The Wagner*

Operas, referred to "the law of two-thirds," citing the climax of the *Lohengrin* prelude as a prime example.) It doesn't have words. It is basically abstract, a matter of design and placement and energy, of line versus space.

"I think a solo should tell a story," Hawkins once told the critic Stanley Dance, "but to most people that's as much a matter of shape as of what the story is about."

I am listening to Eric Dolphy's alto saxophone solo on "Stormy Weather," from 1960, recorded with one of Charles Mingus's groups, about three and a quarter minutes long within a thirteen-and-a-half-minute track. What comes out of Dolphy, above everything else—and there is a lot of everything else, knowledge and study and fundamentals—is something nonmusical: desire, curiosity, confidence, radiance.

Dolphy was, at the time, like John Coltrane, a repeater of his own licks, as if by figuring out six or seven uses for one of them in a single solo he would make it sound more inevitable. Perhaps this leads you back to bird science again: maybe he was practicing a kind of neural self-strengthening, or a way of saying, "I am the person who announces himself by this pattern."

Yet his playing was onrushing, full of faith in the tumble, the hustle. It was aware all the time of not wanting to go in predictable directions. Dolphy was the kind of artist blessed, or cursed, with desiring to make a kind of art that wasn't necessarily desired or asked for among his most respectable peers; he was the kind of artist who wanted to put things in the wrong boxes, somebody who wanted to play in the best bands but in a manner not based on what those bands had previously sounded like. His mentor in Los Angeles, Buddy Collette, many years after Dolphy's death, said that he "loved being different, altering chords. I'd give him a couple of melodies, and he would alter everything . . . He loved all those strange notes to the point of being out there even when the tune didn't call for it."

Ballads calmed him: they let him relax his outpour and opened him up. There are no recordings of him covering "Body and Soul," but surely he was influenced by Coleman Hawkins, particularly in his use of distances between notes, dynamics, dramatic entrances and exits. He was as great a musical actor as Hawkins, in a different style.

In his "Stormy Weather" solo he acknowledges the slow rhythm of Charles Mingus and the drummer, Dannie Richmond, by intuitive reference, playing a series of ideas that wrap around it like a tetherball on a pole, swinging out far but anchored at the base. His relationship to the beat so strongly suggests a dance performance—I am thinking of one I saw once, involving Rihanna and Chris Brown, in which Rihanna stayed stationary while Brown danced around her as if magnetized—that it is hard not to write about it as motion rather than as sound.

There are many pauses for effect, breaks in Dolphy's own projection. This is a kind of oratory. There are huge jumps: in dynamics, in range of pitch and range of tone, the shape and cut of the sound coming out of his horn. The proof of his study comes through in things that he had clearly practiced: arpeggios through chord movement; slow, bending notes; fluttering arpeggios simply repeated but carefully articulated so that you can hear every note in a storm of them; triplet-pattern phrasing and blues cries adapted from Charlie Parker ballads (in which you can hear aspects of Parker's great solo on "Parker's Mood"). But Dolphy pushes them out there with the certainty that his unusual story can be told along traditional narrative lines. He is running not on a typical harmonic grammar but on some other force: urgency and technique. He's aware that he's not just there to fill a space. He's there to say, "I arrived, by your invitation; I told you something important; and I left." And in the middle he's making a list. He's creating a pile of ideas. Some of the world's greatest stories are lists. Often they aren't even thought of as stories.

Jimi Hendrix did something similar in his solo on "Machine Gun," with his trio Band of Gypsys, ten years later. Like Dolphy, like Charlie Parker, and like Coleman Hawkins, Hendrix knew how to make an entrance. "Machine Gun" is a vacant lot, simple as any locus of a great solo could be: a talking one-chord blues in medium tempo, more or less a repeating riff, and when the riff stops, an open space for saying whatever you want to say or playing whatever you want to play.

Hendrix's first note is twelve seconds long—twelve seconds!—repeated once in the middle, a sustained B flat, made liquid and throbbing by whatever combination of amplification and pedal he may be using. (That throb, like the *whup-whup* of a propeller, is so much a part of this note that it becomes an aspect of his tone). It's an alarm, the same kind of effect Eric Dolphy used at the beginning of a solo: it clears your mind for the rest.

As the solo goes along it becomes of a piece with its rhythm-section background: repetition (like the bass vamp), throb (like the bass drum), unbroken sibilance (like the hiss from the ride cymbal). It is constant sound until the end, organized and massaged. Hendrix often incorporated the whammy bar, in small degrees, into his playing, but here, after a minute of the solo—at 5:00—it becomes a concerto for tremolo and pitch-warping, both through his fingering, string-bending hand, and through hard pressing on the whammy bar. Near 6:00, two minutes in, the solo reaches its highest note—the rule of two thirds—and then Hendrix starts to wind down. He dives to the bottom of the instrument's pitch range for a while, playing circles and loops, kicking up dust. He rises in pitch, gradually, and concludes on a screamed chord, before the next section of the song begins. It's been three and a half minutes—about the same length as Dolphy's solo on "Stormy Weather."

A solo is an expression of tone and feeling, or motion, as Hanslick might put it. Its material doesn't have to be wholly improvised. Sometimes interpretation is enough. Iannis Xenakis's pieces for solo instruments presented a fair compromise of these two ideas: they were composed, but with such difficult instructions that the instrumentalist was forced into individual expression in order to make the trip. This is an example of improvisation that can be suggested only by written notes.

His "Mikka," written in 1971, has a relatively slow tempo marking—60 beats per minute, or one beat per second. There are many, many sixteenth notes in it, attached in runs with legato markings, and there are many quarter tones, or notes between our standard notes. But there are no bar lines; where the runs are broken up, there are no rest markings, so the musician must interpret what that means, what the quality of the stopping really is. Halfway through, there are large intervallic leaps, still with legato marks, which means that the violinist must jump between sixteenth notes spaced more than an octave apart.

The composer wanted something specific. But the composer also, without explicitly saying so, wanted the musician to interpret. The mechanics of "Mikka" call on the musician to do things that don't come naturally to her, and also to do things that do. The demands of the piece at first look cruel, then encouraging. As a violinist-commenter on the musicians' message board bangthebore.org put it, speaking of the score: "First thing a violin player says is, 'no, fuck off. Don't be stupid, fuck off.' That's exactly what I said. But it isn't as impossible as it first looks."

In funny ways, this piece—usually about four and a half minutes long—has dynamic similarities to Hendrix's "Machine Gun" solo. It does a lot with the juxtaposition of a long held note and a busy, scrabbling patch; its legato rises and dips connect with Hendrix's control over his pitch, via fingers and tremolo bar. It's trying to get at something about motion relative to stasis.

An improvisation can step beyond the condition of a musician telling the listener "This is what my instant song sounds like." It is a simpler and more fundamental idea: "This is what my instrument sounds like." Some improvisations are a demonstration of sound possibilities from the instrument itself, or gear, or of what hands can do on an instrument. One recording I hear as related to both pieces, Xenakis's and Hendrix's—almost a perfect combination of them—is the album *Ghil*, by the cellist Okkyung Lee, deep and free improvisations with the microphone placed such that you can hear the squeaking and rubbing of horsehair, skin, and wood on the string.

I don't think I know a more fingers-in-materials, physical and textural record made in real time, through the process of improvisation. The word "granular" has become common in referring to a minute focus; this record really does sound granular, as if particles of something are falling into the microphone, or as if Lee wants to reduce her music down to one vibration at a time. Sometimes the sounds are overmodulated into the microphone, or overdriven through an amplifier; sometimes the limitations of a cheap recorder is the reason for the crude, tactile noises. (It was recorded partially outdoors by Lasse Marhaug, a Norwegian musician and sound artist.)

The track in *Ghil* that holds up to a certain type of deep listening—patient, ready for something whole and complete, in search of narrative and dynamics—is "The Space Beneath My Grey Heart." You hear some introductory chords and flurries, fast glissandos not unrelated to the interval jumps in "Mikka," perhaps as a courtesy to the listener, or an assurance: *I know what I'm doing*. Then her aim becomes clear: to make music with no tone, just texture. Using different bowing and fingering techniques—for instance, pressing down hard with the bow using both hands on either end—she brings you into the process. Finally rubbing is all you hear—fast and tiny and frantic, or slow and exaggerated and voicelike, making a spectral glide, a wah-wah effect, as if the individual sounds were vowels and she were shaping them with her mouth. And finally she opens up into chords, as it were, though it's unclear whether she's fingering the neck at all. She's found some sort of slow, stately bowing pattern involving all the strings, with a low drone note. A repetition, and a narrowing of focus away from chords and back to a single tone, brings her out.

What you're doing, when you're listening to *Ghil*, is living between the strings, under the bow. Because of the nature of the recording—there is no room tone, no imagined distance between you and it—you are made aware of how much goes into the production of a single sound. You start to notice where improvisation starts and how it flows as an impulse with the shortest possible circuit: brain to hand to instrument to ear. "The music can even be about the instrument," said Derek Bailey.

Bailey, the guitarist, is the unseen force in the triangulation of Hendrix to Xenakis to Lee. He played alone, or with other people, but after his early years was generally improvising at all times. "I think I've purchased fewer than half a dozen records in my life," he said, on a posthumous release called *Words*, in which he spoke his improvisations rather than playing them. He preferred not to be guided by a text or a pattern, although he candidly acknowledged that never playing with one at all was impossible or at least impractical. ("The idea that nobody in the world of free music plays a melody is pretty outdated," he said sometime in the '80s.) He was at the center of a European movement in the 1970s that seemed to be making up for lost time; he saw behind him the refinement and commitment in jazz improvisation, from tonally organized to "free," more than fifty years of language building, yet he didn't feel part of that tradition per se. He saw the connections between improvisation in jazz and improvisation in other cultures: Hindustani music, flamenco, Baroque monophony and Renaissance church-organ playing. He was interested all the time in improvisation as a proposition, almost as a metaphor for communication. He called himself "influenced, seduced might be a better word, by potentials, or possibilities, things that might be." And he was formally against group-thought or what he called, in *Words*, "fads and fancies." He admired courage, but he was basically a pipe fitter: one sound to another.

For Bailey the sound of multiple hands on instruments and the friction that arose among them—various musicians invited to make moves against one another's potential—was the whole story. Songs were secondary, or unimportant. Though improvising takes public nerve, he could make it seem a shy person's fantasy: anything's fine, as long as it's a music that reflects you, and expresses your listening. What resulted, from him alone or from the ensembles he joined, often seemed a record of his listening as much as his playing. It came out as attention, suspicion, charisma, serenity, perversity, inarticulacy. On *This Guitar*, a record made in 2002, three years before his death, he improvises on a large-bodied and loud acoustic guitar, a 1951 Epiphone Emperor. And he plays his battery of ideas—clicks, harmonics, playing below the bridge, creating chords of the same note, sudden breaks into chopping jazz rhythm guitar. In listening to it, you are confronted with a fluid language built of opposing forces: the hesitation and the knockout emphasis. It's very personal, this recording, which puts you at ease, in the sense that you're not wasting your time; you're listening to someone confident in what he's trying to do, and not bothered about whether that skill can be measured by traditional means. It's much like someone's spoken voice. Curious—isn't it?—how the spoken voice is undervalued as an instrument. There are so many virtuosos of it walking around, wherever you happen to be.

In his confidence, Bailey—the opposite of a traditional notion of a virtuoso—could provoke some of the same feelings as the flamenco musician Paco de Lucía, who played guitar with an aggressive technical commitment, full of articulate runs so fast they barely seemed within the normal constraints of the fingers and nerves. I am listening to Paco de Lucía's *En Vivo desde el Teatro Real*, to the track called "Tarantas"—a traditional form of improvisation, often performed with a singer, based on a particular opening chord, a predetermined mode, and a predetermined set of chord changes, but no set rhythm. The fact that there is no set rhythm means that the musician has license to make any small portion of it balloon and explode.

Tarantas are the laments of miners in Almería: about loneliness, accidents, living with uncertainty. I notice how its smashed opening chords, harmonically fixed except for the moving and dissonant low notes, recall Derek Bailey—both in the way Bailey would make a rude sound to wrest your attention (which recalls Eric Dolphy, too), but also in the way he would push a meaningful sound a little beyond what it seems that it can do: de Lucía is pressuring that chord, digging at it, seeing what's underneath it.

In effect, de Lucía is mining that series of chords. Carmen Linares has made tarantas a fixed part of her repertory, and on a live recording from 2011, *Remembranzas*, she performs one with the guitarist Miguel Angel Cortés. Her opening is a series of guttural moans, for forty seconds. She is working those sounds for as much as they can give her. There are violent shakes in them (much like Hendrix's whammy bar). There are pitches bent into quarter tones (like those in Xenakis's composition in "Mikka"), but she's giving us texture, the gruffness of the voice, as much as notes (like Lee in "My Grey Heart"). She organizes a paradoxical drama of hopelessness: being radical and risky while enacting the condition of having no options.

And here we are, projecting a lot onto Carmen Linares, using words of emotion to describe the quality of sound. Is this how she really feels? Not necessarily. But she invites from the listener an attempt to understand her musical character, or her ritualized movement within a certain form and discipline. An improvisation does say something about the musician playing it—through the hives of choices it expresses; through its limitations and ambitions and echoes; and how the musician arranges elements of sound and reacts to her surroundings under pressure, under threat of failure, or embarrassment, or the music simply ending. We are always looking for ways to extend our lives. There is no better way to research one's own survival than to pay attention to someone else's.

COLEMAN HAWKINS, "Body and Soul," 1939

CHARLES MINGUS (WITH ERIC DOLPHY), "Stormy Weather," from *Mingus*, 1960

JIMI HENDRIX, "Machine Gun," from *Band of Gypsys*, 1970

IANNIS XENAKIS, "Mikka," 1971, Irvine Arditti, violin, from *Chamber Music 1955–1990*, Arditti String Quartet, 1991

OKKYUNG LEE, *Ghil*, 2013

DEREK BAILEY, *Words*, 2011

DEREK BAILEY, *This Guitar*, 2002

PACO DE LUCÍA, *En Vivo desde el Teatro Real*, 1975

CARMEN LINARES, *Remembranzas*, 2011

14. Eyeball to Eyeball

~~~~wwwwlillilliwwww~ Closeness

Those who write about music are generally concerned with contrasts, because contrasts seem to be anecdotally measurable. This is big, that is small. This is rough, that is smooth. We translate sounds into visuals, and we apply our own rulers and meters.

But the sound of closeness—two or more musicians, or musical elements, acting in the purest coordination—tends to escape us because we can't see it. In singing or in playing, it gives the listener a secure, jacketed feeling. Closeness is developed over time, and its value to the ear is absolute.

Closeness is why the drummer Earl Phillips makes so much sense playing shuffle rhythms on records with Jimmy Reed and Howlin' Wolf. Phillips was sensitive and straight to the point; he hooked into his lead musicians and ensured his closeness to them. He built his rhythms out of simple elements: bass drum, snare, and high-hat, and often not all of them at one stretch. Often, as on "Where Can You Be" it was only the snare drum, confidently placed behind the two and four. On "Little Rain," all he had to do was to play ka-*chunk*, ka-*chunk*, ka-*chunk*, brushes on snare drum, something small and sure and enough to give the song its beauty.

Particularly playing with Reed, he had to keep the fish on the line. Reed sometimes sounds wobbly, not in control, or pulled in different rhythmic directions. In "Little Rain" the sound of his shoe tapping the ground is profoundly out of time; the closeness in the track runs between Phillips's drum and Reed's guitar, hands, and voice. At his worst he could sing like the words didn't mean much to him. The reason these records worked when they did has much to do with Earl Phillips— because Phillips gives you the sound of heroic attention. He makes you realize that someone is animating these songs with constant thought. His playing gets inside the singing and strumming, as if grafted to them.

Phillips did something similar with Howlin' Wolf. His limping pattern on "Evil" is one of the great rhythms in popular music, a unit built of a simple sequence: snare, high-hat, snare/bass drum (*ta*-boom), high-hat. It sounds fragile and upside down, full of silent spaces, and its charm is like the little dip, or break, in the Antillean dance step, the emphasis on the two-and-a-half: one-and-two-AND-three-and-four-and. With Wolf he's less part of the foundation than a brace for it, or even an add-on to a work in progress, as in "Smokestack Lightnin'," when you feel that Wolf could have been playing the song for a stretch before he got there. Phillips's job is to jump on the running board at the right moment and lock in. He makes the rhythm sound small and strange; he contains the song. He's swallowed it.

"Entrainment," in biomusicology, describes two oscillating bodies vibrating synchronously, creating resonance. It is one organism adjusting internally to another. It's what fireflies do when they flicker in tandem. When musicians create a functional counterpoint or rhythmic pocket, or when singers sing harmony correctly, without falling off pitch, that's one kind of achievement; but when two musicians of any kind are synchronizing on the surface levels and the deeper ones, too, that's something else. It's often what makes a good performance great, and what makes a certain kind of listening experience great.

Close-harmony singing can be exhausting to the ear, because it puts little value in space or alternation or opposing rhythmic qualities.

All the audience really wants of a close-harmony act is the voices singing together in long tones, the activation of the blend. The bluegrass duo Jim and Jesse—such as on "The South Bound Train"—had the trick down elegantly, similar to the Louvin Brothers but less needling; Jesse McReynolds, the high tenor, wasn't quite as much the lead as Ira Louvin with his brother Charlie. Certain kinds of good singers can feel the internal pulse such that they don't need anyone keeping rhythm with them. And certain pairings of singers are essentially two instruments pulling together to create one resonance. That can be where you join them as a listener.

In the records made since 2006 by the Cuban singer Pedro Luis Ferrer, he has worked with his daughter, Lena Ferrer, and their vocal harmony sounds baked together, then cooled: they seem impossible to separate. They space themselves apart with a lot of major and minor thirds, nothing too unusual—as on "Mi Camino"—but their great breathing-together closeness reveals itself to you through real-time fusing. (They can sound like two notes struck together on a twelve-string guitar, or a tres, though one not restricted to unison or octave-apart tunings.) The father sometimes lets the daughter lead in harmonies, or at least the clarity of her voice pushes outward; sometimes she's tracked as a third voice as well. Even then he doesn't completely recede. They're always together.

The late Beatles sold the notion of four distinct minds, attitudes, tones. But the earlier Beatles, through *Help!*, contained the marvel of closeness between the voices of Paul McCartney and John Lennon. They knew its power; they celebrated it, were celebrated for it, could hardly contain it, may have been frightened by it, may have tried to frighten each other with it. They saw the effect on audiences of singing "ooh" in harmonized falsetto—maybe entrained falsetto—in "She Loves You," and after 1963 traveled further down that road.

I'm listening to "When I Get Home," recorded in June 1964, one of the most carnal, least patient songs of their early period. Its repeated feature is Lennon and McCartney singing the syllables "whoa-oo-oh-*eye*," ending on the first person, or the sense of vision, or the open scream. (The "eye" is a harmony built of a minor sixth interval, the same interval that makes up the first two notes of the guitar introduction to "In My Life.") The song marauds you: voices jumping out of the gate, the drums an announcement of three knocks and then a cymbal crash, and a half-beat before the first proper "one" of the rhythm falls into place. The cymbal crash is the door opening, then Lennon and McCartney spill into your house.

In 1964 they'd reached the mature phase of what the musicologist Ian MacDonald called "eyeball-to-eyeball" harmonies. From that point they started to put learned distance on that skill. When they sang in powerful country thirds in "Baby's in Black," recorded in August of that year, they flattened and nasalized the tone of their voices. Where did they get their closeness from? Perhaps Lonnie Donegan and Les Bennetts. Perhaps Buck Owens and Don Rich.

The Beatles recorded Owens's "Act Naturally" in 1965. Had Owens's band, the Buckaroos, grown more equitably rather than starting as the projection of a single artist, the guitarist, fiddle player, and singer Don Rich would have been understood on an equal footing with Owens; he might have been understood as Paul McCartney. Because together, they had radical closeness. "Sweethearts in Heaven," recorded in February 1963, is a good example. Owens and Rich sing in thirds in the choruses. Rich's voice, taking the higher line, is plummier, as McCartney's was compared to Lennon's. But the synchronization of those voices! On "Saw Mill," from the same period, again with duets on the choruses, they fit together inside the pronunciation of each phrase and each word: the hectoring staccato of "Howya gonna please 'er?" and the quick, two-part vowel in "sa-aw" and "me-yull."

Where did Buck Owens get his closeness from? According to his own stories, from Mexicans singing in the California labor camps where he and his Texan family worked during the summers of the early 1940s.

Listen to the 1940s recordings of Maya y Cantú, Mexican singers who played every day on the radio in XEDF in Nuevo Laredo. (They accompanied themselves: Jesus Maya also played bajo sexto, and Timoteo Cantú played accordion.) It's representative of the music that Mexican workers in California would have known. The two voices travel through songs such as "La Voz de Mi Madre" and "Tengo un Amor" throughout, not just in choruses, the top voice booming and shimmering with vibrato, the bottom voice dryly tracking the phrase rhythms and harmonizing a third below.

Sometimes the closeness of two musicians within a band is what makes the band capable of moving beyond normal limits. The connection between them becomes the power source, creating enough energy for the rest of the band to feed from or mirror. John Coltrane and Elvin Jones had that sort of connection. You can hear it in "One Down, One Up," recorded in 1965 at the Half Note club in New York. Much else is happening in the band: the pianist McCoy Tyner listens hard to Elvin Jones, and plays his version of Jones's behind-the-beat, Afro-Cuban-accented, effectively orchestral rhythm; the bassist Jimmy Garrison orients his lines somewhere between Jones and Tyner. But moving through it most strongly and clearly are saxophone and drums, babbling and rolling. About eleven minutes into a twenty-seven-minute performance Tyner drops out. A few minutes later Garrison does too, and then the listener has the luxury of hearing Coltrane and Jones together, by themselves, for about sixteen minutes.

Jones's cymbal beat lodged deeply and grew within Coltrane's fast-tempo rhythmic sensibility; by this time, five years into their playing together, that spatial relationship to Coltrane's sense of time is part of Jones's musicality, as physically natural as the way a person walks. Jones's constantly scrambled equation of ching-ching-a-ching comes first, and the accents of the snare drum follow; the bass-drum accents follow from the snare, pushing into the formation of the next unit of cymbal beat, like a cycle completing itself. Coltrane phrases with regard to Jones. Jones phrases with regard to Coltrane. When Coltrane starts to phrase continuously, a hurtling and rolling occurs on the drums. When Coltrane's phrasing grows tight and clipped, Jones's rhythms grow crisp and rocking. When Coltrane raises up and whinnies, holding a long high note, Jones holds a press roll. They take a few minutes to arrive at their symbiotic peak—maybe five—and then it's as good as it gets; a listener hears them as one bicameral consciousness.

Coltrane-and-Jones units don't happen very often. They do miraculous things; they can also pull bands apart, or ensure power struggles. The ideal among musicians that a listener perhaps most easily returns to is family, a shared and sharp-eared understanding of musicality down to the level of breathing. Bands these days may have too little time to orient themselves toward the kind of concordance that allows for one fluctuating, real-time imagination to flow into another. (It takes time even more than money, but because both resources are scarce, bands too often must move through circumstances rather than linger in them: their songs, their concerts, their tours, their contractual obligations, their interviews.) Perhaps it happens in jazz more than any other kind of music, though there are plenty of examples outside of jazz: Gillian Welch and David Rawlings, Johnny Thunders and Jerry Nolan, Alla Rakha and Ravi Shankar. And Eyehategod, from New Orleans.

Eyehategod plays rock as a kind of sauce that has been reduced and left to burn in the pan. What's left is thick, bitter, and uneven. It sounds like recalcitrant electric blues, with patterns to be felt best in real, sustained time rather than in flickering exposures. It is not a time-saving proposition, this band, and listening to it means an investment that may not promise quick returns. (There is unresolved screaming in it, and imagery that can only be described as negative—death, sexual abasement, drugs, pain.) It doesn't represent a good business model. But after more than twenty years it has reached a point where it sounds as if the musicians aren't playing this music as a choice or a style, but rather as a basic function or expression of living.

In November 2013 I watched them play in Brooklyn with a new drummer, Aaron Hill, who had after twenty years replaced Joey LaCaze, the only other they'd had. And it seemed clear to me that Mike IX Williams, the singer, and Jimmy Bower, the riff-producing guitarist, were creating, in their own way, a music out of closeness comparable to Coltrane and Jones, or Shankar and Rakha. They were the foundation of the group's slow rhythm and overall sensibility; they were the battery and barometer, with Bower as the definer of the music's general mass and area and Williams as the voice and attitude and maker of particulars. They rarely stood more than a few feet from each other, and they kept the music lying back and hanging open, always waiting to be scooped up by the next syncopated beat. (Does it matter that Williams was born in High Point, North Carolina, where Coltrane grew up, and that Bower grew up in New Orleans, straight south from Vicksburg—where Elvin Jones's people came from—on the Mississippi River?)

Certain kinds of music are built around close partnerships almost as a philosophical imperative, some kind of this-is-who-we-are ethic of sharing or of cultural survival. One kind is jam-band music, in which not only two guitarists but two drummers are not uncommon. Forget about the Grateful Dead for a minute—or refer to them elsewhere in this book—and focus on the Allman Brothers, who are different, and have perhaps been, in a variety of ways and for a convincing number of years, the better band. In the Allman Brothers, both pairs—guitarists and drummers—play in a kind of parallel, but the drummers do it for significantly longer than the guitarists. The best work of that band represents a miraculous vindication for the possibly wasteful idea of having two trap-set drummers in a rock band.

It sounds salubrious to hear the drummers Butch Trucks and Jaimoe play a shuffle together on "Done Somebody Wrong" and a two-step on "You Don't Love Me," both on the record *At Fillmore East*. But often one of them, usually Trucks, will lead, playing all the ride-cymbal hits and the downbeats, because someone always leads. And Jaimoe does a lot with what appears to be a less complicated role: filling the openings. He's like a housepainter doing touch-ups, not on the second day of work, but as the first coat is applied.

This opens the question of why it may be that nearly every experience I have had of hearing double-trap-set drumming has been extraordinary. I am thinking of:

- Sonny Sharrock in 1988 (Abe Speller and Pheeroan akLaff).
- The Henry Threadgill Sextett in 1988 (Reggie Nicholson and Newman Baker, I think).
- Pere Ubu in 1989 (Scott Krauss and Chris Cutler).
- B.B. King in 1997 (I don't know who).
- Joe Lovano in 1999 (Joey Baron and Idris Muhammad).
- The Boredoms in 1999 (Yoshimi P-We and ATR).
- Isotope 217, in 2001 (John Herndon and Dan Bitney).
- A Jason Moran–Robert Glasper double quartet in 2011 (Chris Dave and Eric Harland).
- Kylesa in 2011 (Carl McGinley and Tyler Newberry).
- Kamasi Washington and the Next Step in 2014 (Tony Austin and Ronald Bruner).
- A lot of Allman Brothers and Grateful Dead concerts.

I suppose I might expand the idea to include Ahmad Jamal's band with a trap-set drummer and a hand drummer, and all the Afro-Latin bands I have seen with the same setup or two hand drummers. And I suppose I might add examples I heard only on record in the 1980s and '90s: Adam and the Ants, John Coltrane, the Fall. It seemed for a while there that having two drummers play together was the guarantor of the music I most wanted to hear. Could it be because drumming is *meant* to be done in a unit of two or more, forming a kind of choir, and for purposes other than just music alone? Could it be that whenever two drummers play together on a bandstand, one of music's most basic purposes is uncovered: not an out-front meaning but an inside-underneath-between meaning, to rally and solidify and build a community?

Whenever two drummers play the same rhythm together, we can immediately see what music was before the mediating forces of a culture made it into art. And maybe it's not just two drums playing a single rhythm together. I think of two or three saxophones: the saxophone sections in bands led by Duke Ellington and Woody Herman and Omer Avital, or the long, intertwining lines played by Lee Konitz and Warne Marsh. I think of two or three trombones: the sound of Mon Rivera's early '60s music, of Eddie Palmieri's La Perfecta band, of Willie Colón's records in the late '60s and '70s, and of Colón's *There Goes the Neighborhood*, his collaboration with his mentor Mon Rivera— a record of line-on-line resonance, of radical, loud, and joyous closeness. Maybe it's two anythings playing a single anything together, as long as they're not *trying* to project two distinct styles. Of course they are doing so anyway; they can't do otherwise.

JIMMY REED, "Where Can You Be" (1960), "Little Rain" (1957)

HOWLIN' WOLF, "Evil," 1954

PEDRO LUIS FERRER, "Mi Camino," from *Rustico*, 2005

THE BEATLES, "When I Get Home," 1964

BUCK OWENS, "Sweethearts in Heaven," "Saw Mill," from *On the Bandstand*, 1963

MAYA Y CANTÚ, "La Voz de Mi Madre," "Tengo un Amor," 1946–49

JOHN COLTRANE QUARTET, "One Down, One Up," 1965, from *One Down, One Up*

EYEHATEGOD, *Take as Needed for Pain*, 1993

ALLMAN BROTHERS, "Done Somebody Wrong," "You Don't Love Me," from *At Fillmore East*, 1971

ADAM AND THE ANTS, *Kings of the Wild Frontier*, 1980

THE FALL, *Perverted by Language*, 1983

Lee Konitz with Warne Marsh, 1955

WILLIE COLÓN and MON RIVERA, *There Goes the Neighborhood*, 1975

15. Just a Little Bit

~~~~~~~~~~~~~~~~ Loudness

The world is getting louder. What was once a voluntary or special effect in music is now atmospheric and nearly fixed. Players and listeners are intensifying music because it's not loud enough to be distinguished from ordinary loudness, or taking unusual measures to defend themselves against it.

Loudness represents modern human history—the forces that increase, whether or not you want them to. It is war, factories, and television. Silence, or a richer sound at lower volume, is no longer a state of nature but an insulation worth paying for in the form of vacations, conservation societies, sensitive stereo systems, and concert halls administered by nonprofit institutions supporting a noble idea that is, like most noble ideas, hard to explain to children. Silence signifies the protection of art forms deemed important. Deemed by whom? Not by governments and not by popular opinion, but by critics and those who speak aloud about taste. I am one of these people. One of our powers— if it is ours, if we choose to use it, and if it is a power at all—is an abstract one: to advance the notion that silence, or at least dynamics, is good for us.

In 1976, *The Guinness Book of World Records* listed the Who as the loudest band in the world. The designation seemed important for the band: the Who used loudness for reasons of aesthetics and vitality.

Pete Townshend, the guitarist, said to a Leeds University student magazine reporter in 1970, at the time of the band's *Live at Leeds*: "Our act depends a lot on athleticism, it demands high volume. Even if the group ever gets quieter we will always want voices loud, sounding huge and exciting."

There's a direct link here between "volume" and "exciting." There's also a satisfaction in having done effective branding work. Never mind the Guinness listing, they'd created a generalized mental link: you think of volume, you think of the Who.

But that was a long time ago, and now most people agree that loudness has no artistic value in and of itself. Michael Gira of the band Swans, formed in 1982, whose opinion would be of interest—some have ranked Swans louder than the Who—has said of the band's early concerts: "it wasn't about being loud—that's moronic. It didn't have any aggressive intent. It was more about the transportive quality of volume. I wanted it to destroy my body." That sounds like a more philosophical intent than the Who's: almost a rejection of excitement in favor of something like research or self-analysis. That's a long way to travel in ten years or so.

The late-'50s rock records hadn't been so loud, anyway. Not like Phil Spector and Motown records from 1963 to 1965: songs with big drums and echo, songs made in driving towns, to be heard in the backseat, competing with the rushing wind. The famous Motown beat, as on the Four Tops' "Same Old Song"—with the snare drum starting on the one—drove the overall volume level up, creating fewer dips. It was a strategy for making loudness legitimate. The next step would be making it necessary, as a means of temporary abduction: forcibly trapping the listener, immobilizing him, bringing him inside the music.

And so came *Live at Leeds*, the album, but more important, the concert. And, starting in late 1967 or so, Blue Cheer and Led Zeppelin and then Kiss. At first all this was almost certainly a result of measurable power and technology: bigger paydays made possible through the market optimism of record companies and concert promoters, and a bigger sound made possible through more recording channels. It became evident through the English-speaking world that music wasn't made for and by small communities anymore. It had global ambitions if it was any good. Loudness became a new form of colonialism: it assumed no-fault ownership of an audience's hearing for the rest of their lives. If everything worked out, each audience member had been given a new measure of herself in relation to the vastness of sound. If it didn't work out, at least the band had left her with a medical condition.

Later, by the '80s, loudness became actual aggression: the subtext of spirit-ritual was turned into either attack or sacrifice. And later still it had no meaning at all: loudness just became an unquestioned professional standard.

Many things in the world are loud without specific information to support their loudness—that is to say, loud without their own reasons or set of aesthetics about loudness, without a sense of personality around the loudness. Concerts these days by an emotionally soothing band such as Head and the Heart at quaint, midsized theaters in New England are loud. Movie trailers can be almost vengefully so. A city bus revving up from a stoplight easily blots out all other sounds. (I know because I am writing these words by a window thirty feet from an urban stoplight.)

Blue Cheer's "Just a Little Bit," on the record *Insideoutside*, from 1968: there's the music itself, how it may have sounded at close range, and then the representation of it on record, which is so loud that loudness seems to be part of its intrinsic meaning. More so than Hendrix, more so than the MC5, more so than whatever. Its loudness is its greatness—perhaps not smart, but definitely not dumb. The loudness contains information. The loudness is coding.

Silence doesn't exist, as John Cage found out when he went into an anechoic chamber at Harvard University, probably in the early 1950s. Similarly, loudness is subjective, what the ear perceives; it is not measurable by a machine. (Sound intensity and sound pressure are measurable by a machine.) And it's relative, of course. There are many kinds of loudness: indoor and outdoor, high ceiling and low ceiling, gain versus volume, a high mix versus a high mastering. But even in reduced circumstances you can tell that "Just a Little Bit" is loud, and in a way that still seems like a new gift.

The album was recorded, as the title indicates, both indoors, in proper studios, and outdoors, on various piers and beaches in New York City and Sausalito and Muir Beach. Why outside? The record that preceded it, *Vincebus Eruptum*, was itself characterized as very loud; the legend of the band began to rest on that. Where do you go when you've made what people liked to describe as the loudest record in the world? How can you top it? You crack the shell, you get outside the container. "The San Francisco–based band," according to a 1968 *Go* magazine article written in the tonality of bought or beholden journalism—"uses six amps, 12 speakers, and a double set of drums, and the studio hasn't been built that can perfectly hold their sound." (Six amps meant three Marshall stacks each for the bassist, Leigh Stephens, and the guitarist, Dickie Peterson; a double set of drums meant two bass drums. Had the group really tried every existing studio? What would it mean for a studio to "perfectly hold their sound"? Et cetera.)

A founding member of the band, Eric Albronda—present in 1968 as a newly installed manager—has more recently written online that the record "was an experiment really to see how the sound was near water." There is a subset of compositions written expressly to be performed or recorded in or near water: they include Handel's *Water Music*, John Martyn's "Small Hours," John Luther Adams's *Sila: The Breath of the World*. By contrast, the *Insideoutside* project implied that the group felt it had no other option: it had grown too loud for any enclosed space, too powerful for the normal process of recording, and possibly dangerous for other citizens of planet Earth. And so the best idea was perhaps to record on a platform in the middle of the ocean, with the observable universe as its studio. But *because that was not possible*, recording at the edge of the water became the only sensible compromise.

In an excellent contradiction, the outdoor tracks on *Insideoutside* contained overdubs as well, made in the terrestrial studio—second guitar lines, mostly, power-gunk impasto, strangely out of scale with the rest of the sound—and perhaps there was something to the layering of those different signals, outside and inside, that make its loudness sound so arresting. There is no such thing as loudness. There is only weird or surprising loudness. The records since the turn of the century that have most often been described, and criticized, as objectively loud—Metallica's *Death Magnetic*, the Red Hot Chili Peppers' *Californication*, the Black Eyed Peas' "Let's Get It Started"—are mastered loud from start to finish, processed to contain minimal dynamic range between what were their quieter and louder elements. Those records are blaring. Beethoven's symphonies are dynamic, but Blue Cheer's "Just a Little Bit" is loud.

A loud record reveals itself as loud over time in the process of listening. It steps up to you and pulsates, like a strong setting on a showerhead, rather than flattens, like someone sitting on you. Not just once in a while, according to a formal principle, but a lot, according to feel.

Some of the best examples of loud music were 1960s pop and country and Latin records. These records were made by extraordinary musicians who had learned about tone and projection from the experience of street and nightclub playing, and were designed to blow through the available technology—transistor radios, car speakers, portable record players. You could isolate the aspects of their loudness, and the particulars made an impression: Lloyd Green's steel-guitar leads in Johnny

Paycheck's singles from the mid-'60s, such as "Motel Time Again" (Paycheck's voice itself on those records, piercing in certain vowel sounds, certainly learned from Hank Williams's projection on lines "You'll cry and cry" in "Your Cheating Heart"); the twin fiddles in the Sir Douglas Quintet's "Texas Me" ; the clattering drums and double-tracked singing in the Creation's "Making Time"; Mon Rivera's three-trombone frontline in "La Cuca"; the Sonics, whose singer Gerry Roslie's screams in "Have Love Will Travel" are equivalent in signal-distorting force to the sound of the drummer Bob Bennett's snare-drum hits (a combination that derives from Little Richard's "Keep a Knockin'"); Lou Reed's guitar solo in "I Heard Her Call My Name"; Ronnie Spector's voice in the Ronettes' "I Wonder." The loudness on these records is loud but not totally eclipsing. You can see around the sides of the loudness. You can negotiate your engagement with them.

There are various theories as to why loudness was reduced on records in the mid-1970s: more tracks for recording, which necessitated studios with lower ceilings to contain the sound of individually recorded parts; more album-based home-stereo listening, in which a listener's attention had to be paced over the course of a twenty-minute side rather than a three-minute single; a change in mood and a war-wearied desire for music to be soothing rather than alarming; and the simple reason that record companies and popular musicians made more money in the 1970s, and wealth and quietness go together. Then came punk. The Sex Pistols' first three singles were pretty powerful, but their fourth, "Holidays in the Sun," from 1977, attained genuine loudness.

Punk reacted to the sound of wealth. And so the volume increased until the aural signature of an effective punk song was one that began on a snort of feedback, the sound of loudness beyond regulation. Black Flag made "Rise Above" in 1981, with one of the greatest introductions a song ever had—four bars of Roberto Valverde's swinging two-beat rhythm and a tiny bit more than a quarter note of Greg Ginn's guitar feedback before the riff started. Flipper barreled through entire sets with feedback ringing continuously, even through breaks between songs, the squeals changing like spirit motions.

Dance music doesn't have to be loud. The Loft, a New York dance club run by David Mancuso, has been famous for creating a sound atmosphere that doesn't become aggressive. Started in 1976, it still operates occasionally, according to Mancuso's sound-design specifics, with seven Klipschorn speakers, each a bit over four feet tall, surrounding the dance space in something like a capital M formation. The writer Andy Beta described the Loft's sound recently:

> It is immersive and crystalline, revealing details in records you might have heard a hundred times on earbuds, but it is not loud. The bass does not concuss your insides, and your ears do not ring with tinnitus the next day. Numerous times, we found ourselves able to have a conversation in a regular speaking voice, even while standing right in front of one of the Klipschorns.

You need open spaces in music, real valleys, to talk through it while standing next to the speaker, and Mancuso created his not only through speakers and their arrangement but through the music he chose: mellow and medium-tempo, nothing frenetic, often songs that used congas over a drum set, loosening up the wall of sound and insuring a volume limit. (For congas to be useful, music must be quiet enough to accommodate them.) So: Harold Melvin and the Blue Notes' "Wake Up Everybody." Dinosaur L's "Go Bang." Eddie Kendricks's "Girl You Need a Change of Mind."

Dancing is a form of communication, of course. But just as the Internet promises communication but often delivers isolation, communication amid dance music has changed, especially because of side-chaining. Originally, side-chaining was purely practical: a digital audio device in which one signal automatically lowered when another signal appeared, like alpha and beta dogs. It was useful for DJs speaking over music, or voiceovers in commercials. In dance music it's been used as a great effect here and there—such as in the break of David Guetta and Sia's "Titanium," where Guetta used the kick-drum beat as the alpha dog and the rest of the music as the beta. But in that break, on top of all the bass and synthesizer chords, he also used a significant amount of white noise: pure enveloping hiss. So you're hearing a horrible sound retreating in pulsations, as the kick drum beats it away. There are no open spaces left in the music. It's like a reversal of the joke about why you hit your head against the wall: it feels so good when you stop. Here, the act of hitting your head itself (or, really, the kick-drum sound hitting your head) becomes the relief.

The words describe resilience: Sia sings of being a superwoman, able to resist any abuse; she won't fall, and has transcended an interest in retaliation. But the song itself is a bully, and spells out with its first lines exactly why others that imitate it are too: "You shout it out / But I can't hear a word you say." Do those lines seem so apt because, in fact, nobody can communicate over this song?

The white noise, I think, is the song's most awful aspect—both in the old sense of "awful," and the newer one. Most people remember a frightening and formative encounter with loudness. Mine was in 1983, watching the hardcore band Jerry's Kids, from Boston, at CBGB, in New York. I'd seen Swans by then: subtle by comparison. Perhaps my hearing has never been the same. The two guitarists used feedback— or feedback used them—but that was incidental, or accidental. There was a sound intensity coming from the entire band, through the club's powerful overhead speakers, and it seemed to grow, inching up bit by bit until it became frightening, even without feedback. I understood the phrase "white noise" as a kind of hiss unrelated to music—the sound of channels between stations on VHF television, or the sound you hear growing and receding under the bass-drum thuds in the "Titanium" break. But this experience suggested another application of the phrase. Certain kinds of music can become so overpowering that you can no longer make out their shape: they become almost a dry, smooth sound, like a hanging muffler dragged along a snowy road. I saw the band working furiously, but couldn't hear a note, a word, a melody. It wasn't comfortable, though it made sense in context. The audience was in motion, running and diving and jumping, as one runs in a rainstorm, but nobody had anywhere to go.

Another encounter, experienced in adulthood but not without primal fear, was watching a rehearsal of the Mangueira Samba School at a warehouse in Rio de Janeiro, in 2001. This was unamplified and a matter of mass: dozens of drummers playing high-pitched frame drums and chanting melodies. And also of reverberation, from the hard walls of the building.

And another relates indirectly back to Blue Cheer. It was watching Keiji Haino sing and shriek through two microphones at Issue Project Room in Brooklyn in 2013. Haino is almost a theoretician of loudness: even alone, with just his voice, he can give you something that distinguishes itself, something you remember amid all the other loudness in your life. This is the most shrewd part of his art. The easiest and most self-indulgent part of it is when he sounds like Blue Cheer. (Volume means different things to different people, and as a young man Haino fed the sound of Blue Cheer through an understanding of Japanese student riots and Buddhism.) Fushitsusha is his version of an electric power-trio band; it goes wherever he wants it to go, and across its large discography can at times be fairly quiet.

I am listening to a track called "Secret Black Box III" from a recording of a seven-hour Fushitsusha performance on December 13, 2003, at Hosei University in Tokyo. (Haino is in for a pound.) On this twenty-minute track, after about six minutes, during a nation-sized guitar solo—his standard setup involves two reverb pedals and four amplifiers—I think, This is the one: the loudest record I have ever heard.

The key to Fushitsusha is that Haino is extravagantly loud, aggressive but maximally gestural, and the amount and variety of reverb makes his sound seem bigger than it is. He makes music of great

effort, charisma, and expression, an act of theater and athleticism—
Townshend's word—as much as music. Crucially, to the listener, the
loudness always appears to be a choice. He is interacting with space,
and he is quite specific, not blurry in his decisions. The band, always,
follows him empathetically. His bass players in particular remain in
synch with his every downstroke. And so the effect of hearing "Secret
Black Box III" is one of space but also of loudness; loudness makes
it even more extraordinary, through an almost spiritual power—if we
mean by "spiritual" that which intimates other planes of thought and
refuses definition.

But weren't we just saying that quietness is the sound of power?
In practical, daily terms, yes. But art often works in the opposite of
practical and daily terms.

THE WHO, *Live at Leeds*, 1970

SWANS, *Public Castration Is a Good Idea*, 1986

FOUR TOPS, "Same Old Song," 1965

BLUE CHEER, "Just a Little Bit," from *Insideoutside*, 1968

METALLICA, *Death Magnetic*, 2008

RED HOT CHILI PEPPERS, *Californication*, 1999

BLACK EYED PEAS, "Let's Get It Started," 2004

JOHNNY PAYCHECK, "Motel Time Again," 1967

HANK WILLIAMS, "Your Cheating Heart," 1952

SIR DOUGLAS QUINTET, "Texas Me," 1969

THE CREATION, "Making Time," 1967

MON RIVERA, "La Cuca," 1961

THE SONICS, "Have Love Will Travel," 1964

LITTLE RICHARD, "Keep a Knockin'," 1957

VELVET UNDERGROUND, "I Heard Her Call My Name," 1968

THE RONETTES, "I Wonder," 1964

DAVID GUETTA and SIA, "Titanium," 2011

FUSHITSUSHA, "Secret Black Box III," from *Secret Black Box*, 2003

16. R.S.V.P.

—∿⸺ Discrepancy

I would like to borrow the word "discrepancy" from the musicologist Charles Keil, who has written a fair amount about what he calls "participatory discrepancies."

He described them, in the essay "Participatory Discrepancies and the Power of Music," published in 1987, as "the little discrepancies between hands and feet within a jazz drummer's beat, between bass and drums, between rhythm section and soloist, that create the groove and invite us to participate." Elsewhere: "The two-trumpet sound developed by Marion Lush and now utilized by most polka bands . . . is powerful, I believe, because the blended harmonics of two trumpets guarantee textural participatory discrepancies and a bright, happy sound that invites people to get up and dance." More, to the same end: "in Cuba it seemed to me that the best dancers were consistently 'between the beats' in their footwork."

What was Keil saying? He was saying that those discrepancies are both caused by participation and cause more participation. He was saying, in a sense, that those discrepancies are openings for us to fill and live in—as players, for sure, and as listeners, too. But it seems important that there be an element of surprise or uncontrollability in them to work.

In 1982, Phill Niblock Midwesternly titled his first album *Nothin to*

Look at Just a Record, and the music represented a controlled example of the power of discrepancy in music: a relative closeness among musicians in which the small differences, the ways in which the pitch or rhythm does not line up, become the power centers of the music.

The cover bore out Niblock's title: words alone in blocky type. But a booklet inside described the intent. I am trying to avoid taking dictation: this book is about the listening experience, and therefore about resisting factual descriptions of what the composer desires you to know regarding a piece of music. But here, because the circumstances are so unusual and mysterious—it's hard to know how and why this music was made—it seems like a good idea to offer some supporting information before describing what it sounds like.

The music inside was composed by Niblock and performed by James Fulkerson, the trombonist. It is a tape piece—that is, a piece whose the real composition takes place after the raw sounds are recorded, not before—and a careful realization of Niblock's intentions. Fulkerson blew single-pitch long tones through the instrument, over and over, and Niblock stitched those single-pitch tones together with old-fashioned razor-blade tape editing to get rid of the trombonist's breathing spaces. There are twelve pitches in all, layered and staggered precisely in the editing. To make a nice, resonant, chordal sound, three of those pitches are A, in three different octaves. But above each A are several other pitches, two to four cycles per second higher. (Pitch is measure in cycles per second, or hertz.)

Depending on which octave the A is in, that two-to-four-cycle difference in pitch could mean nearly a semitone or half step on a piano keyboard, or a much smaller interval—something closer to a quarter of a semitone, or an eighth tone. In "A Trombone Piece"—all of side A—you hear some tones that are noticeably far apart, and some that are extremely close. And between each pair of close notes you hear a ghost note—what is called a "difference tone"—which you experience as pulsations. The pulsations recede as the tones get closer together.

And perhaps now you understand how Niblock achieved it, but the point is that when you listen to "A Trombone Piece" you are hearing an intrinsically powerful layering of three trombones and a sense of a chafing between the tones, a difference that seems to imply a vacant lot, or a sense of possibility. (Mon Rivera, Puerto Rican pioneer of the all-trombone brass section, would have been interested.) Something is *off* there, and it's always off in a different way, a living way. The offness becomes a port of entry for the listener; and then, in a sense, it becomes the only thing to listen to.

Through postediting tape assemblage and his choice to use a single player, Niblock overrode a lot: pausings for breath, gulps for air, the possible differences in tone among three different trombonists. He decided to use a single player, multitracked. But he still decided to use a real musician rather than a synthesizer—as Eliane Radigue had done in pieces such as "Triptych" that also used difference tones. I wonder if it wasn't to capitalize further on the idea of difference. Difference tones between two notes that are almost the same are scientifically measurable. But musicians playing almost the same thing together, or playing together toward a common goal, can get beyond measurability. Their little differences can become endlessly provocative; they can amount to the tune that outlasts all other tunes.

The nature of the difference tones in Niblock's "A Trombone Piece" is that they can't be controlled. And such is the nature of the discrepancies between the trombones in Willie Colón's *Lo Mato*, played by Colón and Eric Matos, from 1973—the entire record, but especially where Colón and Matos play lines in unison, the same notes, on tracks such as "La Maria" and "Todo Tiene Su Final": you hear crackings and phase effects as the notes come together and pull apart. What a complicated sound. What a magnificent sound.

(Let's stop and consider something for a minute. We are describing the virtues of voices coming apart to create a loose agreement; we are making an argument against perfect synchrony. That might be postmodernist twentieth-century-ism: a way of thinking that assumes the breakdown or the rupture of a unified whole to be the most exciting and valuable aspect of a piece of art. But the flip side of that idea is two voices *coming together*, yet leaving the agreement loose. This is heterophony: various melodic lines creating essentially the same thing but allowing for differences. This is the tradition of American Sacred Harp singing; this is one of the routes to *tarab*, the concept of ecstasy in Arabic music.)

In the classical-music tradition those discrepancies appear more rarely, because most notes in classical music are meant to be played as written and in tune and because notes are generally hit on top. A planned discrepancy can be magisterial—like the six pianos in Haas's *limited approximations*, tuned in twelfth tones and ringing against one another, playing giant ensemble chords with overtones beating against one another like the largest out-of-tune piano in the world. But outside the classical tradition is where discrepancies have become music's great source of energy.

There are many distinctions to *Patato & Totico*, the record made in New York in 1968 with Totico Arango singing over Patato Valdés's percussion, accompanied by Arsenio Rodríguez on tres, Cachao López on bass, three players on claves, and a five-man vocal chorus. It is the closest thing that the 1960s New York rumba community—an exile Afro-Latin culture that regularly gathered to play in public spaces— had to an authoritative document. It was beautifully recorded, produced by Teddy Reig, the man who'd overseen Charlie Parker's "Koko" session in November 1945—the best distillation of bebop on record, and among the first fifty items selected for the Library of Congress National Recording Registry. It is one of the final recordings by Arsenio Rodríguez. *Patato & Totico* has depth and space; it has rhythmic density; it has quietness and loudness; it has authority and intimacy; it has transparency. But it has so much discrepancy that you can disappear into it.

Its tracks are poetic rituals, not like most of what we listen to in this world. They're street-rumba tracks, but they're untrue to street-rumba reality: they are not field recordings or standard, flat, fast-and-cheap documents. They include a guitarist, or actually a tresero: categorically an ingredient not normally heard with rumba, and specifically the best tresero ever to have lived. (Possibly the best bassist ever to have played Cuban music, too.) There are some unusual levels of intent at play here. There are many ways to hear this record, but the most success I've had is through headphones, at night, walking through heavy crowds in Times Square, smelling street food, visually processing the lights. The record and the neighborhood are complex, knowing places, where nothing happens in perfect synch or in a straight line; they are masterpieces of flickering, jostling particulars, loosely orchestrated, semiconcurrent.

In the album's "Agua Que Va a Caer" you hear Patato's fast conga phrasing anchored by a two-and-three rhythm marked by claves— one-two/one-two-three—with a lower-note conga hit on the first "two," but just slightly, definitively so, ahead of the beat. Then Totico's singing commences, with the repeated downward four-note passage, swinging every syllable: "*Malo tiempo, yo no quiero . . .* " From the start he is almost changing the discourse categorically: he starts *in the middle* of the rhythmic phrase, rather than at the beginning of a new one. This tells the listener: Nothing is fixed, but we have a system; here, instability is strength. It is also, as Keil would put it, an invitation.

As a singer Totico is loose, amazingly loose. He's rushing a little, but remains essentially free, using the placement of the beats only as a reference for what he wants to do. "*In mi soledad*"—he seems to run through that last word, clamping down on it and then hearing the silence blow through the song as the guaguancó rhythm continues. "*Angel divino*," he sings, beginning right at the start of a rhythmic phrase this time. He shoots upward with the melody, and now he's free in a new way—he can phrase as he wants. Thirty seconds into the piece, and he has established discipline over it.

In an alternate take of "Loving Cup," from the Rolling Stones' *Exile on Main Street*, the players sound tired but highly suggestible. And here there are strange, powerful confluences of discrepancy in loaded moments.

For example, the first time Mick Jagger signals the emphatic break with the line "Just one drink." Charlie Watts comes to a stop with a high-hat pump, as if something were to follow, not a line-ending snare beat; the pianist, Nicky Hopkins, fails at the beat a little bit, as if his attention has wavered, while playing regular chords through the break. Mick Taylor, the lead guitarist, continues apace but with a slight hesitation at Hopkins's failure. And maybe somewhere around here a flashed group decision took place: we're wobbling, but we're cohering. Let's use it. Let's do more of this.

From that point on Watts is magnificent, loud and authoritatively awkward, using rolls of uneven lengths, or simply describing a wide area of pulse, as good jazz drummers do. All the musicians then become free, coming in meaningfully on vocal choruses and really everywhere else. They're not looking: they've found their places in a wide circle around the beat.

Keith Richards has considerable skill at cultivating such moments with other musicians, moments when they grow into the empty spaces of one another's grooves, while avoiding any strict notion of where the beat should fall. He can be almost ingratiating, like a confidence thief: this is a source of his power. But Charlie Watts, with whom his musical bond is greatest, has a similar leaning toward discrepancy without seeking favor. Richards uses eccentric technique and eccentric affect; Watts uses eccentric technique and flat, almost businesslike affect. "Neighbours," from the Stones' *Tattoo You*, would be nothing without Watts's discrepancies, the way he drags and slices rhythms—specifically, how he deals out his snare-drum fills, stumbling and locomotive and strange. A book could be written on how many of the best moments of the Stones' music after 1967 come down to slight discrepancies in timing and attack between Richards and Watts, always, and sometimes Hopkins and a second guitarist as well. They are all chattering around the beat; they can do this because they know where it lives. (It lives in Bill Wyman's bass line.)

The discrepant time relationship between guitarist and drummer in Led Zeppelin is part of the key to that band, too. In their best moments—and it does come down to moments, because licks and bravado and pretension usually take over in the long stretch—Zeppelin found a prime energy in rock and roll, the tension between going and staying, desire and responsibility, haste and patience, destroying and loving. The best rock bands of that time suggest movies with a primary link between cool kids and nervous kids: Abbott and Costello, James Dean and Sal Mineo, George Milton and Lenny Small.

"Heartbreaker," the second song from Led Zeppelin's live sets in June 1972—released on *How the West Was Won*—has a twenty-second opening before the singing starts that really is heartbreaking: it moves fast, leaves quickly, and its magnetism seems unintended. The group has just finished "Immigrant Song," and doesn't want to stop. There is a half-second pause, and Jimmy Page plays a pentatonic-scale guitar riff in a hurry. John Bonham enters with his drum groove, just a bit slower, as if to say, *No: this is the proper speed*. Except it can't be that, really. They don't seem to be trying to lock in together, nor do they seem to be trying to miss each other—this isn't stylized beat-rushing or beat-dragging. It is just two musicians running on discrepant interior tempos, being miraculous.

On Sly and the Family Stone's records *There's a Riot Goin' On* and *Fresh*, Stone put an early rhythm machine against a live drummer— possibly not because he was interested in the sonic possibilities of doing so, but because he wanted to work alone. He needed a click track so his songs wouldn't fall apart. The machine was a Maestro Rhythm King; the drummer was often Stone himself, doubled or multitracked.

When you are playing most of the instruments yourself, a useful awkwardness can set in. It is unlikely that you will be equally good on every instrument. There's no cross-playing and cross-listening; on the other hand, you're not deferring to someone else and don't need to codify your song or teach it to anyone. The result is that all kinds of idiosyncrasies can occur. Music can become rich and inspired in its harmonies and its rhythmic demarcations and its pileups of pitch and sound and instrumentation, as in Stevie Wonder's "Girl Blue" (fighting top lines), Skip Spence's "Little Hands" (a tempo that never quite wakes up), Robert Wyatt's "The United States of Amnesia" (long tones, warping drum swing, forgiving attitudes toward pitch in vocal harmonies), and Paul McCartney's "Ram On" (ukulele, Fender Rhodes, choir, bass drum, clapping, whistling.) They can achieve a supreme strangeness, a resistance to the regular order of nature: an inbred quality.

The songs on *There's a Riot Goin' On* are full of discrepancies for a technical reason, too: according to various sources, you are hearing recordings made from master tapes that were repeatedly erased and recorded over in the capricious building of the record, as visitors kept shuttling through Stone's studio and he kept changing his mind about what he wanted. And so you hear actual vacancies: ghosts and erasures, dropouts and mysterious buzzes. I am listening to "Spaced Cowboy." On top of the rhythm machine there are two drum tracks, playing more or less the same thing, but sometimes slightly different. There are two keyboard tracks, one mashed over the other, and he's improvising around the chords. It's strange on the ear: your mind chases discrepant after-beats sticking out from the rhythmic unisons, or follows a single keyboard line for a few bars until it stops cold. Most musicians concentrate on what they have to do as they're doing it. Stone's attention, in each track, seems to be flickering. Is this for himself? Or is it for you? Is he all right? Is it all right that you're listening to it?

Discrepancies abound, too, in D'Angelo's "Untitled (How Does It Feel)," where the guitars and keyboards and kick drum all come together on the one-beat every eight bars, but with a crazy width around the beat. And of course they do in the best of the producer and beatmaker J Dilla, like "Jungle Love," with the rappers MED and Guilty Simpson and the drummer Karriem Riggins, whose backbeat comes down late, a heavy splat, as if produced by something wet thrown on a snare head: drumming by means of cold porridge instead of sticks.

What would these songs be without the slippages of time between the elements lining out the beat—the keyboards, the bass, the drums, the drum machine? This is the question we might end up asking more and more around music not of the classical tradition and not made by machines: What would it be if it were less shaky, more aligned? Are these slippages, even semimistakes, the exceptions to the rule of excellence? Or are they entirely the cause of it?

Sometimes discrepancies can be sought for, studied, and prized. Keil has conducted an unpublished series of interviews with bassists and drummers in jazz, including Vernell Fournier and Steve Swallow, about how they place the beat; they are heroic efforts to figure out what role precision has in the art of being, for lack of a better word, imprecise. (In *Music Grooves*, a dialogue-like book of essays and conversations split between Keil and the musicologist Steven Feld, Keil describes with wonder the findings of Olavo Alén Rodríguez, who conducted a series of "micromeasurements" of drummers' rhythms in performances within various Cuban traditions.) A generation of jazz drummers since the new century has adapted the delayed and sample-imitating beats associated with J Dilla. They sound artful as they imitate the sound of slacking, or of a tape recorder losing battery power. But advantageous discrepancies can also be fast-tracked by limited skill. For instance: the Japanese band OOIOO, who work hard and joyfully at ambitious through-composed music but for the most part do not seem born to their instruments. OOIOO's grooves, in a song like "Polacca," sound the way a three-legged dog looks when running.

This isn't their invention. The trust in wobbly or shallow-pocket rhythm had run rampant in post-punk, from Talking Heads to Delta 5 to ESG. But it also has been the way of groups who best realize their music live, unmediated by the popular music business, to people from a fixed locale or culture (gamelan orchestras, Marion Lush's old polka band), or have other irons in the fire: the desire to be understood as a capital-A artist, or the desire to bring a community together. This is the feeling of playing for small groups of people without interference.

PHILL NIBLOCK, "A Trombone Piece," from *Nothin to Look at Just a Record*, 1982

ELIANE RADIGUE, "Tryptich," from *Tryptich*, recorded 1978, released 2009

WILLIE COLÓN: "La Maria," "Todo Tiene Su Final," from *Lo Mato*, 1973

PATATO & TOTICO, "Agua Que Va a Caer," from *Patato & Totico*, 1968

ROLLING STONES, "Loving Cup," from *Exile on Main Street*, recorded 1969, reissued 2010

ROLLING STONES, "Neighbours," from *Tattoo You*, 1981

LED ZEPPELIN, "Heartbreaker," from *How the West Was Won*, recorded 1972, issued 2003

SLY AND THE FAMILY STONE, "Spaced Cowboy," from *There's a Riot Goin' On*, 1971

D'ANGELO, "Untitled (How Does It Feel)," from *Voodoo*, 2000

J DILLA, "Jungle Love," from *The Shining*, 2006

OOIOO, "Polacca," from *Armonico Hewa*, 2009

17. I Still Believe I Hear

~~~~~~~~~~~~~Memory and Historical Truth

One day in the fall of 2010 I listened to online streams of dozens of bands about to play the CMJ music festival in New York, and I kept hearing the same drumbeat over and over: the one from "Be My Baby."

Historical implications seemed to rise up from the task: When had it been so easy to find the common thread among piles of musicians all over the world in a single day? And as for the common thread, something interesting was happening here: Brooklyn, as we have come to collectively call all American musical culture that prefers not to know where it really comes from, had decided that it was born in a song written by two other people originally from Brooklyn. The song had been recorded nearly fifty years earlier, in 1963, after its writers, Ellie Greenwich and Jeff Barry, had graduated from college, married, and moved to Lefrak City, a brand-new, middle-class Queens tower-block complex. A long time previously, a different world, different circumstances. But the song has allure, does it not?

Listen to "Be My Baby" again, by the Ronettes, produced by Phil Spector. Hal Blaine, who played drums on the session, has explained that the original idea for the beat had been to hit the snare on the second and fourth beats, like a usual rock and roll song, but that during an early run-through he dropped his stick for the two and only recovered it in time for the four: and so was born bass/bass-bass/SNARE.

The action, then, is all bass drum until the four. Sounds like Latin music; sounds like a variant on the habanera rhythm. Anyway: the rhythm doesn't articulate each beat in the bar; it leaves one empty, and strikes between two others. That's what Latin music does. Here is the ghost of the basic Cuban rhythmic unit called the tresillo, which echoes through the Charleston, New Orleans jazz, R&B, early-'60s rock and roll, and reggaeton. It leaves something to the imagination. It's gentle and then violent; it glides you and then shakes you, or rolls you and then rocks you. (The other thing that "Be My Baby" did was to put three loud eighth notes on the four to close out every four bars. *Rat-tat-tat!*) It has something, in a secondhand or known-in-the-bones way, to do with Cuba, which in the early '60s was a very intriguing place, a shadow world—a fire-alarm signifier, a beamer of meaning for Americans and those in the rest of the new world.

It is also a beat that doesn't tell you how you will get to where you're going to go. It just knows that you will get there. It is supremely confident. It is making you write a check without looking at your balance.

Americans and their idolators co-opted and refashioned Afro-Cuban rhythms over and over. The tresillo rhythm is indirectly present in "Be My Baby." It lies more clearly inside Barry Manilow's "Copacabana" and Lionel Richie's "All Night Long" and George McCrae's "Rock Your Baby"; the Bo Diddley beat, cousin to it, is in the Miracles' "Mickey's Monkey" and the Clash's "Hateful" and of course a hundred Bo Diddley songs; the "Be My Baby" rhythm itself animated the Jesus and Mary Chain's "Just Like Honey" in 1985 and then, a quarter century later, Wavves' "When Will You Come" and Bat for Lashes's "What's a Girl to Do?" and lots of others. (The one-man, small-scale singing-songwriting-recording operation DM Stith released a version of "Be My Baby" in 2009 without any drums—a great useless idea.)

The tresillo is general, but the "Be My Baby" beat, like the Bo Diddley beat, was specific. It had its day and then, for a while, that day was

gone. Drummers and songwriters forswore it surely because it inti-
mated a particular kind of pre–Tonkin Gulf Resolution dance, one with
drama and desire and possibility: the opposite of disillusionment. Soon
afterward, the act of playing anything like it would seem naïve and
socially or philosophically backward.

But then what came after it—hippieness—became itself naïve, and
what can you do with these mutually destructive cycles but finally go
with whatever seems to contain musical viability, whatever is built to
last, whatever really knows where it's going?

The beat remains to hand. It never got lost. We love originality
when we can have it, but we can't have it very often. We also love—
nearly as much—that which sounds out of style but stays with us because it sounds inevitable, or touching, or because it solved a problem
at a certain point. "Be My Baby" remains an after-echo of something
in the family of American music that is forever unsquare because it
sees all and presumes to know nothing. The listener feels its kill rate,
senses the presence of a rhythmic virus that burned through centuries
and continents and ultimately became authoritative. You can't condescend to a tresillo. It was there before you got here and will be there
when you leave.

But there is also the atmosphere of "Be My Baby," understood as
philosophy and practice and habitat. There is a handclap strengthen-
ing that fourth beat—you can hardly hear it under the force of the
snare drum, but it's there, implying that this is a street song. There is
the amount of reverb and the possible reasons the reverb was desirable.
(This was during the middle of the golden age of the American middle
class: reverb was a signal of all that democratic bounty.) There is its
mixed metaphor of emotional overkill: the low reeds of big-band music,
the strummed acoustic guitar and castanets of flamenco. There is the
dry petulance and hard New Yorky accent (on phrases like "never let"
and "turn their heads") of Ronnie Spector, her voice opening up into a
swinging-door vibrato at the end of lines. There is her line "I'll make
you *so* proud of me," princessy hokum, a girl practicing a speech in her

mirror. It's self-conscious 1963, a calculation of what will gain traction at a certain place and a certain time.

Imagine picking up a telephone and hearing the distant past: the feeling of the time, the true tenor of things in the air, the striving or modesty or shame of it. You can't do it by listening to "Be My Baby" per se: there you're listening to a product, something complete within itself, well girded, made to be sold, conceived to be perfect.

But you can do it by hearing particular things in and around the distant past.

You can hear it in small imperfections within "Be My Baby" or things that couldn't be rehearsed and faked: Ronnie Spector's accent, the throbbing murk of strings and reeds and background vocals. You can hear it by trying to listen to the drums alone, or one voice alone, imagining yourself at a single fixed point in the studio or the recording space.

This has become easier to do in individuated studio tracks, available on websites here and there—of, say, John Bonham playing drums in the studio while listening to the rest of the track on his headphones (all you can hear is the fantastic whomp of his kit and the tinkle of the rest of the music leaking through his cans) or Michael Jackson singing "Beat It" or Kurt Cobain singing "Territorial Pissings" with the sounds of breathing and of sudden body motions that didn't make it into the record.

You can hear it in the sonic atmosphere, generated through the recording process: here was a person, in such a place, at such a time, rendered by technology that soon may have become laughable. You are hearing the real thing from a real time. You have an idea of what the time was like, because of your own memory, or because you have read or seen historical documents. But this is something different. There is an element of spying going on here: overhearing rather than hearing. This is what we're after when we play (on the drums, or "play" as listeners) the "Be My Baby" beat fifty years later. We want to overhear it. To overhear completely is to possess. We can't possess "Be My Baby" all the way. So when we hear it we can't condescend to it, and when we play it we can only imply it.

The Italian tenor Beniamino Gigli, one of the most popular opera singers of the first half of the twentieth century, became closely identified with the song "Mi Par d'Udir Ancora"—which was an Italianized version of "Je Crois Entendre Encore," or "I Still Believe I Hear," an aria from Bizet's opera *Les Pecheurs de Perles.* He recorded it several times. The 1925 version is to me, for whatever reasons—the focus of sound and performance, and the suspended, uncracking, feminine dream state of his high tenor, even at his climax of "*divin souvenir*"—preferable. In the role of Nadir, a Ceylonese fisherman, he is singing of his love for a priestess he once saw in the city of Kandy. The Italian version adjusts the words a bit for sound value, but the original French libretto says:

> I believe I hear again
> hidden beneath the palm trees
> her voice, tender and sonorous.

Nadir is carried away. "Mad intoxication," he sings. "Sweet dream."

This was, at the time, about as well recorded as recordings get. But there is a mystery and modesty about the performance: despite the best sonic fidelity possible at the time, something about the past is being hidden from us, just as something is being hidden from Nadir. He can't possess the voice of the priestess; we can't possess the song. That recording embodies more than we can imagine, and we can't know it fully. The plainness of the high strings behind Gigli's vocal melody. The amazing slow tempo of it, from a time when people knew slowness— the almost nontempo of it. You can't hear it and say in any definitive way, oh yes, how 1925. It won't let you.

The sound of the drums, from "Be My Baby" onward, is the strongest signifier of time and memory in pop. It explains the common practices for body motion at a certain point in time; it also often dictates how the rest of the music is to be laid out, at the time of creation, and how it is to be heard later on. Listen to the drums, played by Jimmy Carl Black, on the Mothers of Invention's *Freak Out!* and particularly in "Any Way the Wind Blows." They sound far, far away. What a sound. Like "Be My Baby" but more imposing and special, like a statue that must only be seen from a proper viewing distance. It sounds like open air; it sounds like summer. Eight-track recording with tube circuitry, 1966. A time when studios generally weren't subdivided into smaller spaces, when reverb worked as a shortcut to suggest electronic vastness, and a time when many engineers presumably thought all drummers should sound something like classical percussionists in an orchestra— such that you can hear the drum set in full as an instrument meant to be struck loudly and enjoyed, not up close as an instrument meant to obliterate you.

Listen to the enormous drums on Duran Duran's *Rio*, from 1982, especially "My Own Way." You listen and think, well, yes, this is what this group sounded like all the time. But it hadn't a year earlier. Here, every snare hit by Roger Taylor is supersized, a heavy stone splash that should logically displace other sound in its after-report but mysteriously doesn't. This was the miracle of the technologies called triggering and gating. Every snare hit is the same. (On the chorus you hear synthetic drums, which can sound a bit wrong or wanting unless the drummer plays a fill and gets your attention.)

In the logic of this music, large gestures are rewarded. Eighties drum sounds: nothing like them. They were as violently consequential as the invention of reverb or the electric guitar. If you spent a lot of time around them, they stay in your memory. Likely, they changed your hearing. Producers were overcompensating; this was pop's midlife crisis. The numbingness of the drum sound was its charm and its trick. In our great wisdom now we might see this as a liability: nothing wrong with the sound per se, but over and over, on every beat—we don't do that anymore. We mix and alternate and mask; we don't just candidly overdo it. We understand when we hear a record like "My Own Way" that pop had not assumed the size, in an almost physical sense, that its producers and musicians had felt was its destiny; the music, if we can anthropomorphize (and we can and do), was dying to grow bigger, to catch up in sound what it was achieving in dollars. There is such preening and posturing in it. When we hear it we may remember other preenings and posturings—in the way we moved and talked, in our clothes, in our attitudes. That drum sound is both a cause and effect of the way many people were expressing themselves at the time.

And it was trying to address a problem: How domineering can one aspect of the music grow without alienating the rest of it? This is often how music evolves—through innovations that can't be sustained, over-reaches that are inevitably revoked. Another of them was the direct-to-amplifier double-bass sound in jazz in the 1970s. Amplifying the bass directly through a pickup, rather than capturing its natural resonance with a microphone at close range, was for a while a bassist's strategy for keeping up with the greater amplification of everything else. (The sound is primarily associated with Ron Carter, but can be heard even in recordings by more august, pre-1960s musicians: Ray Brown has it on Bill Evans's *Quintessence*.) But listening to these records now, with their rubbery, metallic bass sound—the sensitized strings yield a kind of tap every time a note is sounded—is for some, myself anyway, almost impossible, an irritant of the greatest kind, unless as an exercise in temporal research: a desire to hear the way a certain kind of complex and patient American music was rendered in, say, 1975. The trebly tapping noise seems to vitiate the basic unifying authority of the double bass. It is narrow-souled, the sound of efficiency. Shortly after that period, the pendulum swung the other way, and the sound of the acoustic bass was rendered with almost exaggerated acoustic depth.

Many of us listen through our own memories—not a historical memory, attaching a piece of music to its own time, but a personal memory, attaching it to ours. Sometimes the maintenance of the memory becomes the important thing: we listen, or we don't, according to what we think the memory wants. In the 1980s, my uncle offered to take my grandmother, then living in South London, to hear a performance of the Bach cello suites. She turned down the offer, explaining that she'd seen Pablo Casals perform them, and didn't want another performance to replace the one by Casals in her head.

I suppose I understand this point of view, though I don't quite believe in it. I don't think we have a master tape in our consciousness—the way someone played something at a certain time and place—which becomes the memory's one and only source for a given song. I also don't think that it can be taped over by something else and irretrievably lost. Hers sounds like the refusal of someone whose listening life occurred between the 1940s and 1980s. (Before magnetic tape, you couldn't undo a recording. Nor could you after it went away: the commercially produced CD can't be erased and rewritten; the Internet promises to retain most things forever.) Or maybe she simply thought she couldn't hear anyone play the suites better than Casals and figured she'd be bored—but of course the cello suites, as much as any other pieces of music and more than most, blossom in the mind through hearing successive interpretations. (She would have known that.)

So what would have been her reason for turning down the invitation that way? My best guess is this: she heard Casals; she inhabited the sound of his instrument, and no doubt she remembered where she sat in relation to the instrument; the sound created memory; she lived in the memory, as one lives in a house; she didn't want a new house.

Really, there are two ways we listen through memory—we consult our experience of ourselves, if the music accompanied important personal events or seemed to describe and act upon us directly; or we consult our experience of the music, through our memory of putting ourselves, in one imagined way or another, into the picture of its recording. No matter how much secondhand context we may absorb about a piece of recorded music, we often attach ourselves to it by placing ourselves somehow within it. Sometimes a physical place in that picture seems impossible or superhuman; this can increase our happiness. Imagine where you'd be in the sound pictures of these records:

- Elgar's "Enigma Variations," played by the London Symphony Orchestra and conducted by Sir Adrian Boult in 1970 (you'd need dozens of ears, and to be positioned above various instrumental sections at once).
- Milton Nascimento's *Clube da Esquina*, from 1972 (you'd need to be very close to a guitar in a dry-sounding space, and ten feet from Nascimento's voice down an echoing passageway).
- Kanye West's *The College Dropout*, from 2004 (impossible: this place does not exist).

In the most extreme cases the human has no place in the picture of a song. We are forced to hear as an imaginary anyone, a particle. We can't possess it or create a spatial memory for it. We're listening to a fabrication, a work of electronics and postproduction, made with some kind of attempt—conscious or not, but how could it be unconscious?—to cultivate a bunch of sounds toward the spirit of the time. Your relationship to the song is, perhaps, less with the sound than with that spirit of that time. But still you might remember how you inhabited the spirit of the time, as if it were a physical place.

What are the recordings in which it is easiest to imagine yourself in the picture? Probably bootlegs, field recordings, or one-microphone sessions, of which few enter the stream of mass consumption, like Alan Lomax's recordings for Folkways or Chris Strachwitz's for Arhoolie. As a kid I heard Big Joe Williams's *Tough Times*; and though it was recorded twenty years before I heard it, I placed myself within it. The music flowed through one point in space and time. That point is 1960, Big Joe Williams's living room in Los Gatos, California, and a microphone set at an equidistant point about two feet from his voice and his nine-string guitar. (Surely this example comes to mind because I have not forgotten the Arhoolie album-cover photo, which shows him seated, in recording position, with the microphone set up before him.)

It is a record with lots of imperfections and vulnerabilities. I hear *Tough Times* as a recording from 1960, and can possess it through my own memory even though I was not there—because it sounds like something hearable by a human being at that time, in that room. The slight out-of-tuneness of some of Williams's strings makes it more so.

THE RONETTES, "Be My Baby," 1963

BARRY MANILOW, "Copacabana," 1978

LIONEL RICHIE, "All Night Long," 1983

GEORGE MCCRAE, "Rock Your Baby," 1974

THE MIRACLES, "Mickey's Monkey," 1963

THE CLASH, "Hateful," 1979

THE JESUS AND MARY CHAIN, "Just Like Honey," 1985

WAVVES, "When Will You Come," 2010

BAT FOR LASHES, "What's a Girl to Do?," 2006

DM STITH, "Be My Baby," 2009

BENIAMINO GIGLI, "Mi Par d'Udir Ancora," 1925

MOTHERS OF INVENTION, *Freak Out!*, 1966

DURAN DURAN, "My Own Way," from *Rio*, 1982

BILL EVANS, *Quintessence*, 1976

EDWARD ELGAR, "Enigma Variations," London Symphony Orchestra, Sir Adrian Boult, 1970

MILTON NASCIMENTO, *Clube da Esquina*, 1972

KANYE WEST, *The College Dropout*, 2004

BIG JOE WILLIAMS, *Tough Times*, 1960

18. On the Waves

~~~~~~~~~~ Linking

We love to have music help us with repetitive motion, because there is so much repetitive motion necessary for living. It gets things done. We go to work, we chop the onions, we wash the clothes, we pay the bills, we make the deadlines. Repetitive motion brings us to the end of the work, one motion at a time.

We tell ourselves—and we may be right—that repetitive motion, in large form, cultivates an almost spiritual interest in security or regularity, and guards against chaos. We all want a house and money in the bank. Houses are made of repetitive motions: floorboards and beams, transverses and uprights. Nest eggs are made of repetitive motions: regular deposits.

But music doesn't have to be set at right angles. It does not have to be square or symmetrical or neatly sequential. There are other shapes and motions a musician or band or composer can make to achieve the condition of music, or what the composer Edgard Varèse called "organized sound."

Varèse used that term in an essay that collects bits and pieces of his lectures, called "The Liberation of Sound," published in the journal *Perspectives of New Music* in 1966. The essay speculates about the future of music with an explorer spirit that makes him seem like an astronomer or an earth scientist. He mentions the possibility of seismographic scores and "unsuspected" pitch ranges. But he is also thinking about what drives his own music in regular practice. Music, he explained, comes down to rhythm and form. But both have been misunderstood.

"Rhythm is too often confused with metrics," he wrote. It is not, he argued, a repeated formula of accented beats. It is instead, he said, "the element of stability, the generator of form." (He almost, but not quite, declared that rhythm is an idea rather than a thing, a strategy rather than a set of existing entities.) It "derives from the simultaneous interplay of unrelated elements that intervene at calculated, but not regular time lapses." It shouldn't limit or restrict; it should help create.

As for musical form, Varèse wrote, it is not a structure to be backed into; it is better understood as the result of a process. If the overall form of a piece of music feels obvious and predictable, then the possibility of musical form has been underestimated. Varèse's essay quotes a mineralogist from Columbia University, Nathaniel Arbiter, who shows that the shape and form of crystals start from the shape and form of one internal unit that builds outward. "But in spite of the limited variety of internal structures," Arbiter writes, "the external forms of crystals are limitless."

And that is exactly how Varèse felt about the composition of music. The form must be imposed from the center, not from the outer layers. This, possibly, is how you live when you are not making repetitive motions, when you are entering new problems or encountering elements with a great possibility of variety: you, a being of limited variety, a biped like all the rest, move through these situations, these different rooms of life, each one revealing an endlessly permutating number of changes in color and temperature and sound and feeling. But there is one internal structure that defines them all and makes them cohere into something resembling sense. That is you.

It is well to think about natural processes when we think about music, because music is one of them. Most of us have very little opportunity in our lives to study the formation of crystals, but we may see a fair amount of fire, tide water, feathers, and birds' nests. We know that those things are not simple, sequential, repetitive patterns. And so we recognize implicitly the ways in which certain pieces of music show supreme organization, but seem a result of form cumulatively developed outward from the center, to extend the crystal metaphor—or from the beginning of a piece, since music moves linearly through time. I think about music like this as linking music. Rather than settling within its prescribed parameters, it seems to move inexorably forward and outward, unfolding and enfolding, according to the logic that suits it best.

Gabriel Fauré's piano quintets were composed, in a macro sense, with so-called sonata form: the sequence of theme, development, and then recapitulation. But the heart-destroying slow third movement of his Piano Quintet no. 2, touching down in variations on three melodic motifs—gives the impression of moving forward without circling back to step one, without externally imposed form or square movement. It intimates a trajectory through room after room, each one different, the only fixed element being the consciousness of the composer, or more to the point, the listener. It appears not to have a plan; it pushes ahead and spreads out.

I am listening to the version played by Quatuor Ysaÿe, with Pascal Rogé as pianist. By the middle point we have circled up and up and up, around a hill, building and dropping through volume and pitch, sometimes through harmonized contrary motion. And then at about 6:45 the most curious thing happens.

There is a three-note descending motif, pushed through different keys and backgrounds of harmony, developing slowly and intensely and contrapuntally, its lines entering in overlapped succession like waves of a chorale—or just like waves—until just less than two minutes later, when the air seems to be let out of the piece and the music works toward some kind of resolution. In that two-minute section is an emotional experience that does not reduce to a single word or idea: it only describes the complicated feeling of moving forward to the next station in life, knowing that there is really no other choice, knowing that there may be horrors ahead, but that no two horrors are alike and none are absolute. Perhaps because of its constant and complex chain-linking—of melodic strains, of emotions, of tonalities—it suggests the contradiction and complexity of living: hope and possibility and maybe even some kind of transcendence or ultimate joy, as well as a very everyday dread. Animated by all that possibility to develop, the piece becomes a kind of living organism.

In the end, the piece achieves sublime craftsmanship. But it also promises a deep and complex sense of logic for the listener. Through its echoes, its climbs and descents, its circular patterns, it seems to be saying: nobody travels alone. Nothing is unconnected from anything else.

The slow movement of Fauré's op. 115 connects in my head with "Spiritual," by the Chicago gospel bandleader Donald Lawrence, recorded in 2011. "Spiritual" is, on one level, a catalog of tricks from an arranger and pastor, a double-shift worker in music and religion: Lawrence gives his choir technical instructions, lyric prompts, and homilies as the piece moves forward, showing you both the logic and faith behind his organization of sound. The piece marches in slow funk, a rhythm of sureness; Fauré's lacks any such thing. But like op. 115 it moves in compounding complexity, a strange order of directions, with coordinated brass-section interludes and a couple of bridges, one of them changing keys and tonalities, breaking down and producing complicated colors. More instruments keep entering to produce more counterpoint; each section grows thicker and more intricate as it moves along. He's in charge of getting the band from A to B to C, but none of the parts are perfunctory. He suggests a structure that values A *and* B *and* C. His thoughts and directives link the sections together; they also catalog some of the musicians, generate forward momentum, and intensify the purpose of the whole operation. If one were to hear everything Lawrence says in six and a half minutes condensed into a single paragraph, it would run to about 150 words. It would establish a split focus between the audience—whoever was in the room when the music was recorded, or you listening to the song in your own space—and the band and choir. "How many spiritual people in the room tonight?" he begins. He asks rhetorical questions: "What you gon' say right here?" He tells the singers when to divide into harmonize parts and perform a glissando effect and when to "say it with attitude." He names the horn players. He urges the band to get him closer to the motivating force of the music: "Take me to the book!" His comments form a through-line that doesn't return to a refrain, a narrative of linking.

Arvo Pärt's "Cantus in Memoriam Benjamin Britten" repeats the same motion over and over again, or series of motions: a descending minor scale, overlapping, made longer and longer, with slower-motion parts of that scale moving behind it, against the background of a bell tone and growing tremolos as notes begin to accumulate at the bottom. (Where there is no low register heard at the beginning, the listener becomes increasingly aware of one as the notes begin to pool together at the bottom end of the string instruments and the end of the piece. When the notes are collected there, heaving like bullfrogs, unable to go anywhere else, the piece ends on a last bell tone.) It implies natural patterning, in the sense of patterning that is not only sequential but interwoven—like feathers, like ripples on the water. But also in the sense that it all came from one idea and moved outward to a whole composition.

And the first movement of Henryk Górecki's famous Symphony no. 3 does something related to both Lawrence and Fauré, also through chorale-like means: it starts and ends with figures rendered in deep bass tones, layering more and more figures that are progressively higher in pitch, building a stack of moving parts. The piece creates an atmosphere, a weather that keeps changing and becomes mottled, a mesmerizing and stupefying pattern, with lonely details poking out in the cycles of each layer, a bit like the accent notes played on guitar in Nick Drake's "Road." Unlike the others, it makes a bell curve: it returns to where it began. So it does, to some degree, suggest an outward form. But for most of its middle it generates a constant forward linking, not particularly interested in resolution.

Listen to Dorival Caymmi's version of his song "O Mar," from his 1959 voice-and-guitar record *Caymmi e Seu Violão*. Three minutes and one second. Caymmi is not an obvious representative of this complicated, multidirectional, letting-the-song-grow-its-own-feathers kind of motion. Most of his songs sound so confident, sung in such a reassuring voice—deep and broad and mellow, seeming to resonate in the listener's throat—that they imply instant folklore: they are reports from the sudden forever, the contemporary always.

"O Mar" has a short, straightforward samba in its middle section, one that tells the story of the day Pedro the fisherman never came home from the waters to his Rosinha de Chica. But as a whole it is full of a feeling that the song could go in many directions. It has no fixed tempo, and veers off its course of major tonality. It is a song of the sea, and carries within it something about waves and tide, a quality of time and movement. Its chord changes can be unresolved series of half-step modulations, or deliberate and conclusive. They go where the composer wants them to go; they are not bound by form. They seem to be generated from within.

We've been talking about music that, either by design or accident, communicates great happiness or great sadness. (Sometimes both.) And one could make an argument that those emotions were intentional. One could bring biographical details into it. Fauré's quintet was written after the stress of World War I, between 1919 and 1921, in old age and semideafness, or warped hearing: for at least ten years before its composition he had been hearing the middle register faintly but in tune, while low notes seemed to be lower and high notes seemed to be higher. We don't have to know this, but we do. Górecki wrote a two-way lament for children and parents in wartime. Caymmi praised the sea as the source of great beauty—"*e bonito, e bonito*"—while transmitting its deadliness. ("*Quanta gente perdeu seus maridos, seus filhos / Nas ondas do mar?*"/ "How many people lost their husbands, their children / On the waves?") Pärt wrote a requiem. Lawrence wrote for the glory of God.

These are noble songs. They seem to contain so much of life that is contradictory and that does not necessarily add up: beauty and terror, low tide and high tide, systole and diastole. And they repeat, though not in a simple way. (Sometimes only in a partial way.) They pile up or intersect motifs and tonalities. To some degree they imitate the way we have a compulsion to stay in our joy or our sadness, saying "and then, and then, and then," bumping from one topic area to another, stringing together ideas. We are backing into the subject of emotion again, but there it is. The great linking works seem to be telling you something about the process of living.

Henry Threadgill has steered toward a kind of music that moves along surely, while offering few clues about what kind of goals it wants to reach or how it will reach them. In the work he has written for his group Zooid, the tonality is sure, moved along by strong lines from cello and tuba, both of them standing in for the traditional role of bass. But it pivots here and pivots there. "Tomorrow Sunny," from 2012, is at bottom a series of written intervals, and those intervals have an identifying flavor: they communicate that they have been generated by Henry Threadgill. But the direction of the piece remains unclear from moment to moment. The paths of the various instruments are coordinated, but not all with one another. You can't predict its movements. It winks along with equanimity and teasing and seems to be written in invisible ink: it is a kind of funk without referent, a dance music that nobody ever became expert at dancing to. If you are looking for structural logic, it will bedevil you. If you are looking for an emotional atmosphere, it will bedevil you there, too. Threadgill has his sound-world, his basic melodic-rhythmic idea, his generative center, down cold; from there he builds outward. If you isolate a single musician in the ensemble—any of them, other than the drummer—you are hearing one step to the next step to the next. But together their movements are staggered and interleaved; they don't reduce to a simple sequence.

If you listen to it with a clear head, "Tomorrow Sunny" is inviting music, bright and clear. It integrates lines spaced apart in pitch and timbre—Threadgill's flute on top, above acoustic guitar, cello, tuba, bass, drums—with lots of gaps in everyone's phrasing, except for the drums, which press on with popping dance rhythms.

Those gaps bring the listener in. And when the listener is in, he wonders: Do I know my way around? Do I speak the language? How much of this can I predict? Can I tell when the group has completed a cycle? Can I anticipate resolutions, or peaks, or dropouts? Will I know when it's time for a solo? Do I know how this music means to make me feel? How much, in a sense, can I control?

Less than you think, Threadgill's music answers. It is not forbidding. But it takes that power away from you. Put another way, it relieves you of that burden.

GABRIEL FAURÉ, Andante Moderato from Piano Quintet no. 2, op. 115, 1919–21, Quatuor Ysaÿe, Pascal Rogé

DONALD LAWRENCE, "Spiritual," from *Your Righteous Mind*, 2011

ARVO PÄRT, "Cantus in Memoriam Benjamin Britten," from *Tabula Rasa*, 1984

HENRYK GÓRECKI, Symphony no. 3, London Sinfonietta, 1992

DORIVAL CAYMMI, "O Mar," from *Caymmi e Seu Violão*, 1959

HENRY THREADGILL, "Tomorrow Sunny," from *Tomorrow Sunny/ The Revelry, Spp*, 2012

19. Mi Gente

⎯⎯⎯⎯⎯⎯⎯ Community and Exclusivity

Some of the best listening experiences are the most alienating. You might be a reasonably knowledgeable and well-traveled person (whatever that means), living in a major metropolitan city (whatever that means). You might have a passing familiarity with a few languages, and you might be basically unafraid of looking like you're in the wrong place. You've been the only whatever in the room plenty of times.

Yet you will step into a community temporarily redefined and strengthened by ecstasy in a music that, it turns out, you haven't learned enough about. Essentially you are a child waiting for a stranger to have pity on you and explain the map. You are worrying that you have gotten lost.

But being lost is not an absolute condition. It only means that you haven't received enough cultural information yet. Everyone knows the critical moment, whatever the circumstances, when confusion ends and understanding begins: I'm not lost anymore; I can see the way ahead. The feeling is the same when you can't find your way home in a foreign city or when you have gone to a concert and can't understand why the crowd has started cheering intensely at a beat or a dance. It's not science. It's culture. It's good to experience exclusion. It only means that you can then become part of a community.

Many of us, around music, reach a time when we don't want to learn a new map. We're skeptical. Seems like there's a new map every six months. Do I have to learn them all? Can I count myself out once in a while? Mostly: *Since I know the old map, I should be able to read this one. If I can't read it, it's not worth knowing.* This is the unseen force that obscures the inventory.

There is a messy narrative claiming that bebop was invented in the early 1940s—by the same people, it is supposed according to the myth, who became famously identified with it—in order to create a new and exclusive club dedicated to a revolution in taste and training. Bebop was tricky to play harmonically and rhythmically, and so your inadequacy would show if you weren't ready to sacrifice for it. It was played after-hours at a few clubs in Harlem; if you were a listener in this situation, you'd have to be up into early mornings in Harlem, wanting to see small-band music in a small place, which often meant you were a competitive or curious musician who'd finished your big-band job in a big place. The core musicians, according to the narrative, knew they had a prize, a golden ticket, and it was pure; they wanted it to be neither stolen nor diluted.

There's plenty of this kind of thing in *Hear Me Talkin' to Ya*, the oral history of jazz compiled by Nat Shapiro and Nat Hentoff. Dizzy Gillespie: "So on afternoons before a session, Thelonious Monk would work out complex variations on chords and the like, and we used them at night to scare away the no-talent guys." Kenny Clarke: "As for those sitters-in that we didn't want, when we started playing these different changes that we'd made up, they'd become discouraged after the first chorus and they'd slowly walk away and leave the professional musicians on stand."

Those "different changes," of course, became a sound and a style. But early on they helped engender a new kind of privilege, writing rules for a newfound land, where the creators could monitor the borders.

Over time, the narrative has been revealed as a half-truth: bebop evolved a lot more slowly, and with more desire for commercial acceptance, than these quotations indicate. I have never been sure whether the people who perpetuated the narrative—historians and writers, mostly, arranging the anecdotes in a certain way—felt threatened by the rise of such a club (because exclusivity can create new positions of power and also begin wars), or saw its formation coldly, as an inevitable outcome of human evolution and behavior (many musicians do, after all, believe in a natural aristocracy of talent), or imagined the club as something they needed to belong to.

All music is powered by its search for a membership. Some music seeks as large a membership as seems feasible: perhaps not only young but under forty, perhaps not only American but English-speaking, perhaps not only Mexican but pan-Latin. Some seeks a smaller market, or feigns exclusivity—as if the enjoyment of a kind of music could be patrolled—and operates on the assumption that many more people would like to be part of that group than actually are.

Louis Jordan's "Saturday Night Fish Fry," recorded in 1949, shows you exclusivity and gives you community. It is an idealized step-by-step demonstration of a culture, the culture of young black musicians in southern cities. I am listening to it now and I feel the map being drawn instantly: it tells the listener how and where to eat, how to dance, how to be excited, how to be skeptical, how to live. But first, how to get past the door.

Its narrative is Rampart Street in New Orleans: the song was written, mostly, by Ellis Walsh, a bandleader from there. Jordan—originally from Arkansas but by that time a New York songwriter, crossing from big-band jazz into what would soon be called rock and roll—adapted the lyrics but kept the location. Its point of view is that of the impressionable opportunist, new to the particulars but wise to the patterns: if you want to eat on a Saturday night in New Orleans, if you're "a cook or a waiter or a good musician," you get yourself to a fish fry and you talk your way in. The narrator gains entry to one, and so does the listener.

And then the narrator becomes a roving camera eye, like the tracking shot through the Copacabana in *Goodfellas*: there is Sam jiving with Jimmy's wife, there's a fat piano player, women in expensive dresses or bobby socks. The point is: multiplicity, flexibility, movement, bounce, style, response. (The rhythm tells you all that, and so do the answering riffs on piano and guitar.) There's a police raid. The narrator is hauled into jail and forswears visiting another fish fry, but that doesn't matter: you've been in, you can't undo what you've seen. "It was rocking," goes the chorus. "You never seen such scuffling and shuffling till the break of dawn." The assumption is that you know why the story is worth telling.

The great singer Umm Kulthum, from the 1930s to the 1970s, provided an experience of belonging and participating and identifying to more citizens of the world—chiefly the Arab diaspora—than most performers ever had before. Her performances were exercises in mass identification; they were also social and religious, to some degree. They illustrated a new way forward for Arab thinking: a twentieth-century model that would have to proceed without as much Western influence as had once been anticipated. And so these performances—many of which were recorded—had a more urgent intent than many ever will. "The world represented by her performances," the scholar Virginia Danielson has written, "is where many listeners have wanted to live."

"Ana Fe Intizarak," a live version from March 3, 1955, is a great example—her lines, whether improvised or written, are followed loosely by the string players of the ensemble, and her phrases are bursting, soaring, drenched in emotion but untiring.

These performances are as much as an hour long, and they construct a map, too; they have a logic and a grammar. Some of her stunning long tones don't provoke applause, but some improvised sections, in which the strings mimic her patterns—and in effect show you how difficult she is to mimic—reach the audience deeply; they erupt in applause and chatter and yelling while the ensemble continues. This is the ritual of *tarab*, a kind of managed process of ecstasy in Arabic music.

And their ensembles use heterophony—the concept of variations on a single melodic line coming together in rough agreement, the tool that so much English-language music has ignored outside of rural religious music or amateur choirs. Heterophony in itself implies community: it implies people of different interests moving in the same direction. Listening to "Ana Fe Intizarak" is a serious proposition—its length, its intensity, its coding. It asks you, as Aaron Copland did in *What to Listen for in Music*, whether you are listening to your music correctly; but by that point it has made you complicit in its making.

Some songs are quite clear in how they'll get their membership. The Germs' "What We Do Is Secret," from 1979, opens a little side-door to a private ritual, establishing a general and exciting "we"—the band, perhaps their friends, perhaps their fans. Flipper's "Brainwash" 45, from 1981, makes it nearly impossible, but more desirable, to get inside: the vocalist, Bruce Lose, struggles to begin a song and ends it with "Never mind, forget it, you wouldn't understand anyway." (A locked groove in the vinyl makes the phrase repeat forever.) Héctor Lavoe's "Mi Gente" (my people), from 1975, invites all Latin Americans—"*ustedes*," with the assumption that "my people" and "you" are the same—to get inside. Cultural pride is the ticket. If you identify with him, you're in. If not, you'll never hear his call.

> *Vinieron todos para oirme guarachar*
> *pero como soy de ustedes*
> *yo los invitaré a gozar*
> *conmigo sí van a gozar.*

(They all came to hear me party / but as I am from all of you / I invite you to have fun with me / if you're going to have fun.)

Loretta Lynn overlapped with Héctor Lavoe in chronology as well as sound and temperament: her voice was honest and unapologetic— loud, husky, eager, sometimes clumsy or independent of the groove, with nothing to hide. Her 1971 single "You're Lookin' at Country" wins the hospitality award: it talks straight to her audience, appeals to its visual sense for decoding music, and essentially offers it a guarantee. As long as they know what they've come for, and as long as they know what "country" is, they'll be satisfied:

> I hope you're liking what you see
> because if you're lookin' at me
> you're lookin' at country.

The idea that the audience is looking for something to hold on to and belong to, that they have ideas about membership and authenticity— all this is taken for granted. She's selling herself, but not in a way that compromises who she is.

Deaf Center is a Norwegian duo that plays dark-ambient music— and here it seems worthwhile to break with my attempt not to put the name of a genre in the first mention of a group. The reason not to do so is because it seems a severely limiting mode of definition, as if a group exists only to take part in the construction of a genre. But the reason to do so here is only because Deaf Center really does seem attached to a limited definition for themselves. They are exploring a mood and trying to make it last, whatever the consequences, however narrow the music ends up being.

The mood is sort of sullen, static, natural, invested in abstract beauty: the aural equivalent of, let's say, dark, high-definition, close-up photographs of furrows and fungi. It is achieved by heavily echoed long tones played on stringed instruments—cello or electric guitar—and piano notes, recorded closely but with a microphone capturing their long decay.

There is, in other quarters, some wordless mood music that achieves its goal efficiently: that's what the pianists Jim Brickman and Philip Aaberg do, for instance. Theirs is music about melody, but intensely attuned to the desires and myths of a certain kind of American— sentimental, aging, and well trained by the emotional cues in film soundtracks. It implies with great strength that all is well with the world. Deaf Center does not achieve its goal efficiently and does not bring easy peace. It goes the long way around.

The group's work is amazingly visual, as music can sometimes be: alluringly lit, as if you are hearing shafts of light and blankets of shade. Its reverb and long decay suggest natural patterns and unseen forces. In "Close Forever Watching," from *Owl Splinters*, a plan takes shape. It becomes a tidal shift between two chords, with a thick pressure of sounds growing around it—multiplied human voices, perhaps string notes slowed down or run backward. In any case, it is immersive, beckoning, and not meant to convey anything other than time, voluptuousness, and some kind of rumination. The listening experience is not about the performers, Erik Skodvin and Otto Totland, whose musical identities are obscured either by reverb or by a kind of cold and impersonal playing. It is about you and the mood and the darkness. Are you the kind of person who identifies with this mood? Here it is, at length. If you're lookin' at me, you're lookin' at country. If you don't identify, go to a better-lit place.

The tendering of an extreme mood, in these cases, keeps out the riffraff, the no-talent listeners. Because passive acceptance isn't an option, it makes listeners know that they need to have a reason to be here. And among certain skilled musicians the extreme mood is communicated very, very quickly, by means of a special method. Morrissey, for instance, has his sigh, and had it from the first Smiths single, "Hand in Glove": an exhaling that transmits a weariness and a state of being transported. He doesn't want to be where he is. He's created a willed world more suitable to himself, and perhaps to his fans.

The Mexican ranchera singer Vicente Fernández recorded "Volver Volver" in 1976, and it became his signature in performances thereafter: one of the most extravagant records in pop, the wettest song in a discography drenched with fictional tears, where women tend to be sublime and all sacrifices total. Except for the slow, steady chop of the nylon-string guitar on the two and four, the sounds are doubled or massed or echoed: double trumpets, tremoloed organ, earth-moving strings. He is practicing emotional psy-ops: ending a verse with a soft, plummy, contemplative phrase ("*Y me muero volver*"—"I am dying to come back") and then starting the chorus with an incredible bellow ("*Volver, volver, volver.*") His voice clutches with tears; soon he delivers a fantastic yelped *grito*, the cry of Mexican independence that became the stamp of ranchera: I love my people, I love my song, I'm prepared to die for either—and you? "Ey-aww, ey-aww, ah ha ha ha!"

The ranchera *grito*—as practiced by Vicente Fernández, or Miguel Aceves Mejía—is a wordless marker, a cultural stamp, a sound as good as a slogan. An Umm Kulthum long tone, a Louis Jordan blues narrative, a Morrissey sigh, a Deaf Center echo, are all *gritos* in their own way. They are enticements to join and reminders of a fee.

LOUIS JORDAN, "Saturday Night Fish Fry," 1949

UMM KULTHUM, "Ana Fe Intizarak," March 3, 1955, live recording

THE GERMS, "What We Do Is Secret," 1979

FLIPPER, "Brainwash," 1981

HÉCTOR LAVOE, "Mi Gente," 1975

LORETTA LYNN, "You're Lookin' at Country," 1971

DEAF CENTER, "Close Forever Watching," from *Owl Splinters*, 2011

THE SMITHS, "Hand in Glove," 1983

VICENTE FERNÁNDEZ, "Volver Volver," 1976

20. Slowly Fading out of Sight

⎯⎯᷄᷄⎯The Perfect Moment

In the mid-'80s I went to hear Merle Haggard at a New Jersey arena concert so heavily sponsored by a cigarette company that its operatives gave out half-packs by the beer concessions. During his set he played "Silver Wings," a song with great stillness and resonance and trust in its tonic chord. Space opened up around him in the music: the rhythm section played its parts very quietly.

At one moment, between two lines of lyrics, he strummed a guitar chord in a slow upstroke, from the highest string to the lowest. I stopped breathing and felt as if a splinter were being withdrawn from my skin. Here was a little detail, a trebly chime, so full of meaning and wordlessly consistent with the information of the song—the shiver of loneliness, the glint of the airplane leaving with the girlfriend in it—that it blocked out nearly everything else: it's all I remember.

We think of pieces of music from a distance as blocks of time, but can we hold more than a second or two in our minds? And are we—with all music, to some extent—waiting around for some pinpointed extraordinariness to happen? Not necessarily anything as obvious and mechanical as a peak of pitch or volume, like the swells in DJ Snake and Lil Jon's "Turn Down for What." Maybe we are waiting for what we might slangily call perfection.

In music, nothing is perfect, unique, or exclusive: Haggard, as mannered a performer as Marlon Brando, could have done any number of little things at different points in that song and perhaps achieved similarly strong results. But we will use the term as a figure of speech to denote a particular event.

A perfect moment is often wordless, or indirect if it has words. It is the song blushing: an unplanned or perhaps only semiplanned occurrence in which the music suddenly embodies its own meaning. The conscious mind of the singer or the instrumentalist temporarily goes out the window. It can contain everything of value about the piece of music in one note or chord, or a very short sequence of time. It communicates a complicated human gesture, feeling, or interaction that could not be literally demonstrated or sung; it transcends or surpasses the listener's expectation set up by context in order to create a moment of beneficial confusion or satisfaction. It is the song turning itself inside out for you, sleepwalking or convulsing or speaking a temporary truth.

Perhaps here we're on the thinnest ice of subjectivity. Is my perfect moment your perfect moment? Possibly. No guarantees there. I do know, anecdotally, that many people notice the same ones, given a little training. That's why more than one person cries "Ole!" at a flamenco singer.

Near the beginning of Miles Davis's "The Meaning of the Blues," from *Miles Ahead*, after the introduction, Davis improvises slowly—looking for his own perfect note or moment, perhaps, but only playing at the middle of his game—over a brass-and-reeds background of ascending chords that keeps changing its instrumentation at the arrival of certain new chords. Those backgrounds don't change in a neat sequence, one type of sound switching fully to another—but in staggered swaths, suggesting color gradations. So the climb begins with low brass, then low brass and oboes, then high brass and oboes, then brass and muted high brass and oboes, then—the oboes drop out—muted brass alone, as thin and silvery as Haggard's upstroke.

At the point of muted brass alone—the chord-climb continues for only one more step, in an eight-second sequence (0:55 to 1:03 or thereabouts)—the listener feels at great altitude and in thinner air. During that perfect sequence, Davis plays only two notes, bouncing between them with nonchalant meaning, as if defending a point in conversational speech, first arguing with reason, then driving the point home. You hear that? Not much in what he played required a lot of planning. But as a gesture, his casual top line against the vertiginous background, it feels magnetic, possibly because it suggests a deep human experience—in the sense of human experience as motion—without spelling it out as such. I wouldn't know how you'd read it. For me it suggests a lot at once: futility and transcendence, transitory beauty, maybe loss, maybe a cool face during hot events.

Frank Sinatra was a literal singer: when he wanted to express happiness, he sang like a confident man. When he wanted to express sadness, he sang like a defeated one. Plenty of people may tell you that he sang thousands of perfect notes—at least one in each of his greatest performances. I'm not so sure of that. But once in a while he, too, could create one of these overwhelming, irreducible moments.

The record *Only the Lonely* repeatedly asks *"What'd I do?"* It is about the out-of-body confusion of having been dumped: a man's looping, self-recriminating, self-absolving thoughts. He can only think of himself in one frame: loser. "Good-Bye" is its peak, and the peak of "Good-Bye" is the chorus. It comes around twice. As the chorus builds in admixtures of major and minor, he sings: "But that was long ago." The sound-mass drains away, as does the narrator's courage, and he adds "You've forgotten—I know."

In the first chorus, that addition sounds realistic: he's moving forward with his life, because what are the options? The second time, the swelling builds higher—the "o" of "ago" is the longest-held and most powerfully sung vowel in the entire song, with a mighty vibrato—and the draining afterward more dramatic. Now, when he sings "You've forgotten—I know," in a light tone with little spin on it, he seems temporarily absent, blank. Where is he? He's disappeared into the song. What makes this a perfect moment is that Sinatra performs within the drama of the music, not the emotion of its character: he becomes a faintly ridiculous man in the low tide.

John Lydon, unlike Frank Sinatra, is not a singer concerned with developing a system of expectation and reward with the listener. He's not even necessarily dependable at being undependable: beyond a small number of great and pressurized performances he can come to seem like a collection of trademarks—a monotone chant, a palpating wail. Like Young Thug today, in the '70s and early '80s Lydon was brave and astonishing with limited resources, and left behind some of the most perfect moments on records: he gathered up whatever was the ugly or battling spirit in the music and hurled it out through his voice. Because the Sex Pistols' "God Save the Queen" was the band's greatest antiprogram song, one giant self-destruct button—here's something that monarchies are built to suppress!—it was his perfect song, and as it happened, contained his perfect moment.

The song is, plainly, an attack—on the culture of respect toward the queen, but really toward any monarch—and on the listener. It's like a cousin of the Stooges' "No Fun"—which the Sex Pistols covered—with the same kick drum and snare pattern and similarly patterned vocals, but it's gotten off the couch; it is complaining with a purpose. The band had enough training in outrage, at this point, to know that they had to play a sort of stamina game within three and a half minutes; with the slugging drums, the anthem guitar riffs, the wild, hoarsening leer, it's like a Felix Trinidad boxing performance, in which the stamina seems to increase as the match goes on.

The perfect moment arrives in a preview just before Steve Jones's guitar solo, and as a feature just after it: the return to the one and the tonic chord and Lydon yelling "God save the Queen. *We mean it, man! We love our queen!*" Before: trenchant, surprising, funny. (He means nothing of the kind.) After: all that plus mania. The singer has left the

practical world. He has achieved the correct state of mind for starting a
public disturbance and getting people to join it: he has become magnetic, and it is this song's purpose to find magnetism.

What is "Time," from Sly and the Family Stone's *There's a
Riot Goin' On*, about? It is slow and slouchy. Sly Stone sings as one who
is bothered by the nature of time: his complaint is possibly even bigger than Lydon's, maybe the biggest one humankind has and the
most abstract, the one Proust wrote a seven-volume novel about. It's
a composition, a set of chord movements, but so much of it is delaying
through improvising—voice-and-keyboard, black American church
stuff, melisma and passing notes and wah-wah, putting shapeliness
and swell into the moment now, and now, and now, because at certain
points in life, and in listening, you become anxious about time moving
when you don't want it to. You fall out of step. And so there is no way a
song such as this can achieve greatness unless it demonstrates, in some
extraordinary way, falling out of step.

The first line is "Time needs another minute, at least." The second is
"But you got a limit." And as we listen to "Time" we might experience
some of this two-sided frustration ourselves—that of the person who
needs the world to slow down and hold up, and of the person who's been
waiting too long already.

Its top lines sound mostly improvised, with disjointed emphasis. ("A
bear! / A bear-in-the-woods / Looks forward to hiber-*na*-ting.") The
playing—electric piano, bass, a little guitar, drum machine—is sensitive and beautiful, so much that we want it to keep rolling. At one place,
before a key change, he builds up our hopes with tremolos, as a way of
making us impatient for the next phase, the next target. He delivers
heavily. And at a later place, near the end of the song, he builds up
expectation and then withdraws, dissolves, melts. That's it: that's the
song's perfect moment.

The track was made during a period when Stone was typically understood as a man from whom great things could be expected but who

had started to test that understanding—working in isolation, hard to deal with, self-medicating, revising and rerecording, perhaps not trusting others or himself. (Sometimes he sings parts of the song off the microphone, but there seems like a reasonable chance that the sounds you're half-hearing are the magnetic tape residue from an earlier run-through.)

Stone goes down low and sings another line that doesn't scan to spoken phrasing, stretching out the words, mockingly: "Time, they say—is the aan-*swer*. Huh." Then he yelps quickly, in a falsetto: "But I don't believe them!" And from there—from 2:37, to the end about twenty seconds later—the song begins to crumple and dissolve.

Stone makes a strangulated noise, as if he's run out of ideas, or has been punched in the stomach. ("T-t . . . uh.") And then an appearance of a sound: a keyboard sound, like a church organ heard from down the block. Almost a smell, or a coloring of the sky, more than a sounded tone. You can't quite picture the musician's hand.

Who's playing that? How did it get there? Was it on purpose? Is it a ghost from an old take? Is Stone making it himself? Is he even hearing it? Is he reacting to that noise as we are? Like Sinatra, he seems to have momentarily lost his sense of a man making a recording for others to hear: he stepped inside the song and almost died in it.

"Ask the Watchman How Long" is a song recorded by the Moving Star Hall Singers, a praise-house choir from St. John Island, off the coast of South Carolina. It is about uncertainty and having no resources but the power to ask. It feels liberated by its loud, rough, loose harmony, its intersecting patterns of cracking voices; but it also feels like a work song stuck in place, trudging slowly to a slow underlying single clapped beat: a work song. Life can't go on like this forever. Just before two minutes in the singers seem to rear back and sing in unison: "*How long? How long?*" Suddenly a cousin of the tresillo rhythm comes in and the song begins to jump: a transformative moment of decisive action. The desire in the song has found its target. Because implicit in the question "How long?" is a desire to know time and measure it, to master it; the sudden bounce in the rhythm marks a transition toward that mastery.

~~~~ᴡᴧᴧᴧᴧᴧᴧᴧᴧ~~~~Al Green's "Dream," from his *Belle Album*, takes the shape of a slow dance with very quiet, almost chirping backup vocalists, and a glossy organlike synthesizer setting. It is about perfection—about a generalized version of beatitude. There are no referents: the song imagines a state of grace, not necessarily one created or managed by Green, or the character in his song. It says "make it last forever"; it suggests that you should "dream without knowing the reason why." And at one point the singing quiets down to nearly nothing, as if to show how little one needs to experience that kind of happiness. "Shh, shh," Green warns. "Oh, dream. *Shh!* Dream, dream dream. Dream. Dream dream. Dream. Shh. Won't you dream-dream-dream? Skies are shining bright, oh. Dream—let your mind and your heart just melt, melt, melt like ice— dream. Ooh, ooh, dream."

Then he stops short: maybe he's looking down, concentrating on his guitar. An Al Green song, with Al Green temporarily missing from it. The two backup singers continue their cycle. "We can make it all come true," they chirp, in the deep background. And they do this for four more eight-bar cycles, but it's the first one that is the most perfect because it contains the surprise disappearance. Of course this is a convention: this is where the soul singer shakes hands in the audience, or feigns exhaustion, or enters his transports, while the band vamps and the backup vocalists continue. But this is a song about moving into meaning. Al Green is actually doing it: melting, making it last a long time, seeming to forget the reason why.

~~~~ᴡᴧᴧᴧᴧᴧᴧᴧᴧ~~~~Héctor Lavoe's "Periódico de Ayer," from 1976—written by Tite Curet Alonso, arranged by Willie Colón—is about a woman's love that has cheapened over time, the way a newspaper does; by the afternoon it's forgotten, or "*olvidada*," as Lavoe phrases it with a kind of distortion in the mouth, as if he were tasting something gone off. It's an angry and self-protective song, and the man takes no responsibility; it exacts revenge through metaphor. And because it is about time as an

inevitable force and as natural enemy, the instrumental section in the middle demonstrates the passage of news, or love, through time.

One can imagine both of those narratives clearly: a focused and exclusive communication between lovers, or between reader and newspaper. Then the communications grow complicated: counternarratives from other directions, or other stories muscling in to push the first one out of focus; the appearance of old relationships as threats, lapses in trust, deal-breaking behavior. And then both turn into nonsense— discord, darkness, something to be swept away so a new cycle can begin.

The dramatic part of Colón's arrangement—two instrumental middle sections of a nearly seven-minute song—puts quarreling trumpets and trombones over massed strings. For eight bars a trumpet plays D-G/C-F—a kind of logical statement, a pair of perfect-fourth intervals that, if reversed (C-F/D-G), would echo the "Bring back, bring back" section of "My Bonnie Lies over the Ocean." The trombones seem to talk over it, inveighing against it. The strings enter in unison, like backlighting. A trombone takes up the perfect fourths and the trumpets find their own rejoinder. And then the amazing thing happens: the trumpets go sour. Their harmonized rejoinder moves into dissonance. Nothing continuous or displeasing: just synchronized jabs of dissonance in the brass. (The first of them are the most perfect moments.) The song grows its own poison plants.

━━━━ Betty Carter sang a short song called "I Think I Got It Now" on her live record *The Audience with Betty Carter*. Everything about it is unlikely: extremely slow, yet short; no solos by her or anyone else, yet aggressive improvisation within the simple words in the vocal lines. It isn't vocally normative like Sinatra: it doesn't put the emphasis in obvious places, it's not afraid to confuse the listener. Her text seems clear enough. She is a grown and picky woman who has found a mate and hopes that he might be the one. But underneath the words two forces run together. One is emphatic: *Do you get how good this man is? Am I making myself understood?* And one is tentative: *I have been wrong before and I don't like disappointment, but I am beginning to hope that I can relax into this relationship.* The song implies something complex: that she is looking for a way to express joy and security and isn't sure how to do it. She can only show without telling, by putting the spirit of the song into the sound of the words.

> I think—I got it—*no-ooow.*
> I think I got the answer—for me.
> For me it's you-ou!

There is a lot of qualifying here—"I think," "now," "for me," "someday," "soon." The music she wrote around all of that becomes a slow love song of strange design, with unusual and argumentative chord changes. And in her phrasing there is the usual contradiction of new love: over-excitement and hesitation. She communicates the fragility of hope and trust. It doesn't sound rehearsed. It sounds only like the life force. Is there one perfect note? Yes: the second syllable of "you-ou." Or perhaps the song is one long perfect note.

And then later:

> We'll—
> Be lovers—
> Someday.
> Soo—oon.
> Soo—oon.

MILES DAVIS, "The Meaning of the Blues," from *Miles Ahead*, 1957

FRANK SINATRA, "Good-Bye," from *Only the Lonely*, 1958

SEX PISTOLS, "God Save the Queen," 1977

SLY AND THE FAMILY STONE, "Time," from *There's a Riot Goin' On*, 1971

MOVING STAR HALL SINGERS, "Ask the Watchman How Long," from *Sea Island Folk Festival*, 1968

AL GREEN, "Dream," from *The Belle Album*, 1977

HÉCTOR LAVOE, "Periodico de Ayer," 1976

BETTY CARTER, "I Think I Got It Now," from *The Audience with Betty Carter*, 1979

Sources

Adorno, Theodor, edited by Richard Leppert. *Essays on Music*. Berkeley, CA: University of California Press, 2002.

Bachelard, Gaston, translated by Maria Jolas. *The Poetics of Space*. Boston: Beacon Press, 1994.

Bailey, Derek. Interview with Jim Macnie, archived at lamentforastraightline.wordpress.com

Bailey, Derek. *Improvisation: Its Nature and Practice in Music*. New York: Da Capo, 1993.

Baraka, Amiri. *Black Music*. New York: William Morrow and Company, 1968.

Becker, Judith. *Deep Listeners: Music, Emotion, and Trancing*. Bloomington, IN: Indiana University Press, 2004.

Beta, Andy. "A Night at the Loft, the Dance Party That Spawned All Other Dance Parties" (*Pitchfork*, Feb. 19, 2014).

Blake, Ran. *Primacy of the Ear*. Third Stream Associates, 2010.

Bryant, Clora et al., eds. *Central Avenue Sounds: Jazz in Los Angeles*. Berkeley, CA: University of California Press, 1998.

Burke, Edmund, edited by James T. Boulton. *A Philosophical Enquiry into the Origin of Our Ideas of the Sublime and Beautiful*. Notre Dame, IN: University of Notre Dame Press, 1968.

Cage, John. *M: Writings '67–'72*. Hanover, NH: Wesleyan University Press, 1973.

Caramanica, Jon. "Strong Medicine: The Screwed Sounds of Big Moe" (*Boston Phoenix*, May 16, 2002).

Castiglione, Baldesar, translated by George Bull. *The Book of the Courtier*. London: Penguin, 2003.

Castro, Ruy, translated by Lysa Salsbury. *Bossa Nova: The Story of the Brazilian Music That Seduced the World*. Chicago: A Cappella Books, 2000.

Cavicchi, Daniel. *Listening and Longing: Music Lovers in the Age of Barnum*. Middletown, CT: Wesleyan University Press, 2011.

Chilton, John. *The Song of the Hawk: The Life and Recordings of Coleman Hawkins.* Ann Arbor, MI: University of Michigan Press, 1990.

Copland, Aaron. *What to Listen for in Music.* New York: New American Library, 2009.

Croce, Arlene. *Writing in the Dark, Dancing in the New Yorker.* New York: Farrar, Straus and Giroux, 2000.

Danielson, Virginia. *The Voice of Egypt: Umm Kulthum, Arabic Song, and Egyptian Society in the Twentieth Century.* Chicago: University of Chicago Press, 1997.

Duckworth, William, and Richard Fleming, eds. *Sound and Light: La Monte Young/ Marian Zazeela.* Lewisburg, PA: Bucknell University Press, 1997.

Dylan, Bob. Speech at MusiCares Person of the Year award ceremony, Grammy Awards charity gala, Feb. 6, 2015.

Getz, Michael M., and Dwork, John R. *The Deadhead's Taping Compendium, Volume 2.* New York: Henry Holt and Company, 1999.

Hamilton, Kenneth. "The Virtuoso Tradition," in David Rowland, ed., *The Cambridge Companion to the Piano.* Cambridge: Cambridge University Press, 1998.

Hanslick, Eduard, translated by Geoffrey Payzant. *On the Musically Beautiful.* Indianapolis: Hackett, 1986.

Henahen, Donal. "Reich? Philharmonic? Paradiddling?" (*New York Times*, Oct. 24, 1971).

Jackson, Blair. "Blair's Golden Road Blog—Goodbye to My Cassettes" (dead.net).

Keil, Charles, and Steven Feld. *Music Grooves.* Chicago: University of Chicago Press, 1994.

Khan, Hazrat Inayat. *The Mysticism of Sound and Music.* Boston: Shambhala, 1996.

Kramer, Jonathan. *The Time of Music.* New York: Schirmer, 1988.

Krehbiel, H. E. *How to Listen to Music: Hints and Suggestions to Untaught Lovers of the Art.* New York: Scribner's, 1897.

Langer, Suzanne. *Feeling and Form.* New York: Scribner's, 1953.

Lawrence, Tim. *Hold On to Your Dreams: Arthur Russell and the Downtown Music Scene, 1973–1992.* Durham, NC: Duke University Press, 2009.

Lewis, Miles Marshall. *There's a Riot Goin' On.* London: Continuum, 2006.

MacDonald, Ian. *Revolution in the Head: the Beatles' Records and the Sixties.* New York: Henry Holt and Company, 1994.

Mathieu, W. A. *Bridge of Waves: What Music Is and How Listening to It Changes the World.* Boston: Shambhala, 2010.

Mathieu, W. A. *The Listening Book: Discovering Your Own Music.* Boston: Shambhala, 1991.

Milner, Greg. *Perfecting Sound Forever: An Aural History of Recorded Music.* New York: Faber and Faber, 2009.

Murray, Albert. *The Hero and the Blues.* Columbia, MO: University of Missouri Press, 1973.

Nectoux, Jean-Michel, translated by Roger Nichols. *Gabriel Fauré: A Musical Life.* Cambridge: Cambridge University Press, 2004.

Newman, Ernest. *The Wagner Operas.* Princeton: Princeton University Press, 1991.

Pollack, Howard. *Aaron Copland: The Life and Work of an Uncommon Man*. Urbana, IL: University of Illinois Press, 1999.

Rosen, Charles. *Music and Sentiment*. New Haven, CT: Yale University Press, 2010.

Schaeffer, Pierre. *Solfège de l'Objet Sonore* (audio version of text with sound examples to illustrate the text "Traité des Objets Musicaux," released 1967 by ORTF).

Schonberg, Harold C. "A Concert Fuss: Music by Reich Causes a Vocal Reaction" (*New York Times*, Jan. 20, 1973).

Shapiro, Nat, and Nat Hentoff. *Hear Me Talkin' to Ya: The Story of Jazz as Told by the Men Who Made It*. Mineola, NY: Dover, 1966.

Small, Christopher. *Musicking: The Meanings of Performing and Listening*. Hanover, NH: Wesleyan University Press, 1998.

Szendy, Peter. *Listen: A History of Our Ears*. New York: Fordham University Press, 2008.

Varèse, Edgard. "The Liberation of Sound," from *Perspectives of New Music* 5, no. 1 (Nov. 1966).

Young, La Monte. "Notes to Composition 1960 #7."

Young, Rob. *Electric Eden*. New York: Faber and Faber, 2010.

Acknowledgments

I am grateful to have known the three people most important to the existence of this book: Paul Elie, who signed it up and championed it; Alex Star, who took it over and got all the way in; and Zoe Pagnamenta, my agent—for nearly half my life. Thank you.

Nik Cohn and Allaudin Mathieu heard about this for years before I let them read it. Their insight, skepticism, and encouragement have been crucial.

Thank you to Harold Bott, Jon Caramanica, Nate Chinen, Eric Chinski, Mark Christman, Christopher Dunn (regarding Sonny Carr), Gary Heidt (regarding Curtis Mayfield), Harmony Holiday, Charles Keil, J. D. King, Susie Linfield, Tom Mc-Dermott, Sia Michel, Hankus Netsky, Jon Pareles, Carla Parisi, Marcus Ratliff Sr. and Jr., Michael Robbins, Rob Saffer, Hank Shteame, Ben Sisario, Declan Spring, Peter Watrous.

Index